Family Laugh Lines

by Kathryn Murray

Illustrated by Don Miller

Prentice-Hall, Inc., Englewood Cliffs, New Jersey

To my husband, who grins when he is the butt of a joke and whose own favorite line came from Sam Levenson's quip, "Arthur Murray earns his living by the sweat of his frau!"

Family Laugh Lines by Kathryn Murray

© 1966 by Kathryn Murray

Prentice-Hall International, Inc., London ° Prentice-Hall of Australia, Pty. Ltd., Sydney ° Prentice-Hall of Canada, Ltd., Toronto ° Prentice-Hall of India Private Ltd., New Delhi ° Prentice-Hall of Japan, Inc., Tokyo

Family Laugh Lines And How They Started

In every household there are certain remarks that live on through the years because they apply so well to every day situations. Some of these phrases are the punch lines of jokes. Others come from true happenings but they all become a frequently used means of family communication.

Some time ago Arthur said to me, "There are a great many family sayings with amusing incidents as their background. You should start collecting them—they might make an entertaining book." I answered, "That's not a bad idea. I may do it some day." He asked, fast, "*When?*"

"*When?*" came from the night that we met a friend of ours during intermission at the theater. She talked for the full ten minutes about her new house and as the lights blinked to call us back for the next act, she said, "But you must see it—you must come and dine with us." Arthur's "*When?*" came with such split-second timing that she was left with her mouth open.

Arthur is not the kind of man who sits by idly—not when someone else is hanging around doing nothing. So he kept after me until I did start this collection. Now I'm very grateful to him because I've had so much fun with it and we've adopted many of these sayings ourselves. You may find that you'll be using some of them, too.

Contributors

(in order of appearance)

Alan King
George Jessel
Anthony Quinn
Art Linkletter
Robert Goulet
Sam Levenson
Willie Mayes
Skitch Henderson
Patrice Munsel
Gypsy Rose Lee
Rudy Vallee
The Murrays
Ray Bolger
Leonard Lyons
Victor Borge
Mike Douglas
Herb Caen
Herbert Mayes
Orson Bean
Cleveland Amory
Shari Lewis
Hugh O'Brian
Jerome Beatty, Jr.
Bob Cummings
Mrs. Jack Paar
Dina Merrill
Mrs. David Sarnoff

Guy Lombardo
Ernest Borgnine
Mrs. Kermit Kraus
Jan Murray
The Fredric Marches
The Murrays
Arthur Marx
Lawrence Welk
Groucho Marx
Bert Parks
Mrs. Herman Schoenberg
Ozzie Nelson
Billy Rose
Mrs. Ed. Sullivan
Norman Murray
Henny Youngman
Beatrice Lillie
Virginia Graham
Irving Mansfield
David Janssen
Dr. Joyce Brothers
Myron Cohen
Mark Goodson
Hy Gardner
Marilyn Gardner
Cobey Black
June Havoc

Bil Baird
Edgar Bergen
Myra Waldo
Howard Whitman
Mary Blunt
Art Buchwald
George Burns
Johnny Carson
Norton Mockridge
Zachary Scott
Eddie Sherman
Jack Albertson
Joan Crawford
Dick Clark
Eli Wallach
Anne Jackson
Robert L. Green
Monty Morgan
Bert Lahr

Mimi Benzell
Goodman Ace
The Murrays
Jean Carroll
Peter Lind Hayes
Arthur Treacher
Elaine Stritch
Dorothy Stickney
Judith Crist
William Davenport
Frank Fontaine
Earl Wilson
Ann Landers
Helen Hayes
Merv Griffin
Lady Bird Johnson
Mike Wallace
Rod Serling

Family Laugh Lines

From Alan King

Alan King is a forceful, articulate comedian who enjoys writing his own material. He made his first big impression as a newcomer, back in '56, when vaudeville was temporarily revived at the old Palace on Broadway. He has since become very well-known throughout the country as an often-repeated-headliner on the *Ed Sullivan Show*.

TV appearances are highly profitable for the amount of time they require, but there is incurable ham in every actor and Mr. King yearned for a straight role. He proved to be very good as the lead in the Broadway comedy *The Impossible Years*. His wife, Jeanette, was not surprised. She said, "Alan even plays better tennis when people are watching."

The Kings and their two sons, Bobby and Andy, live in a pleasant Long Island suburb where most of their neighbors have rather large places. Jeanette and Alan have a favorite comment for any richly lavish display.

It comes from the time that George S. Kaufman, of the shaggy eyebrows and sharp wit, was visiting Moss Hart's luxurious country place in Bucks County, Pennsylvania. Moss took his guest on a tour of the estate and proudly pointed out the artificial lake he had designed, the waterfall he had planned and the beautiful effect of landscaping he had installed. Back at the handsome house, Moss asked, eagerly, "Well, what do you think of it all?" Kaufman's heavy eyebrows raised slightly—*"Looks like what God could have done if He had money."*

From George Jessel

George Jessel was dashingly named for a relative, Sir George Jessel, but Georgie and his widowed mother lived on New York's lower East Side where Grandpa had a hole-in-the-wall tailoring shop. Customers waited while their pants were being pressed and little George would come out and sing for them.

Then George's mother wangled an audition for him at a nickelodeon, where he was hired to join two other little boys in a song and dance act. One of the boys was Walter Winchell. The act was billed as THE IMPERIAL TRIO and the theater sign announced: "It's worth five cents alone just to hear little Georgie Jessel sing." Thirty years later, Winchell wrote, "And that still goes!"

George became a handsome juvenile on Broadway, a vaudeville comedian, songwriter, film, play, and book author and Mayor Walker's official toastmaster. He officiated so often that Will Rogers said, "Every time Jessel sees a half grapefruit he automatically rises and says, 'Ladies and Gentlemen, we have here tonight' . . . ."

Mr. Jessel's fluent wit is still heard at benefit dinners and he is still writing books and performing. Early in '66, while entertaining in Viet Nam, he was hit by a ricochet bullet but planned to return there when fully recovered. Here is his description of one of his favorite stories.

"When someone is evasive and I want the facts I say, *Now tell me—I'm Kramer.*'

"The story is that a phone rang in a hospital and when the floor nurse answered a voice asked, 'Can you tell me how Mr. Kramer is feeling?' The nurse answered, 'Mr. Kramer is just fine. In fact, I think he'll be going home tomorrow.'

"The voice on the phone said 'Thank you very much' and the nurse asked, 'Who shall I say called?' The answer was 'This is Kramer—the doctors won't tell me a damned thing!' "

From Anthony Quinn

A Hollywood producer once said, "Anthony Quinn must be crazy. A top star and he's over in Italy making a picture for buttons! . . ." The picture was *La Strada* and Mr. Quinn did it for "buttons" because he wanted to work with the director, Fellini. *La Strada* was a prize winner and the Quinn portrayal was called flawless.

Anthony Quinn is half Irish, half Mexican and wholely dedicated to his work. At the presentation of his second Oscar he said, "I would like to say that acting has never been a matter of competition with others. I was only competing with myself and I thank you for letting me win the fight."

Here is an endearing family story told by Mr. Quinn.

"When my wife and I have a difference of opinion and neither of us manages to convince the other we don't say 'O.K., you're right.' Instead, we use a remark made by our three-year-old son, Franky.

"We were in Miami where I was doing *Mr. Innocent* for Sam Spiegel and Columbia Pictures. I was leaving for location one morning and Franky didn't want me to go. Almost crying he asked where I was going and I said, 'I'm going to work' and I started for the door. He ran after me. 'No, papa, no. Stay with me!'

"I said, "But Franky, I can't. I have to go to work. It's very important. . . . ' He jumped up and down. 'No, it's not important. Stay with me! . . .' I tried to explain, patiently: 'But Franky, if I don't go to work, I won't have any money to buy you toys . . . .' He stood still, thinking and then said, '*You better hurry—you might be late.*' "

From Art Linkletter

Arthur Gordon Linkletter was born in a place with the darndest name — Moose Jaw, Saskatchewan. His first broadcasting job was as Program Director for KGB radio in San Diego. That was when he was twenty-two years old. He stayed with the air waves and now Art's grin is recognized by all regular TV viewers, for the shows that he writes and in which he stars have a huge following. He is known for his books, too, that are best sellers.

Less publicly known is the fact that Mr. Linkletter is an astute businessman with big mogul titles, among them Chairman of the Board of Great Eastern Mines, Director of Royal Crown Cola, Flying Tiger Line, Diners' Club and other enterprises. Early in '66 he went to Hawaii with sizable real estate ventures in mind. He also gives his services to the YMCA, serving on the Board in Hollywood and working on the Executive Committee of the whole Southwest area.

But Art's foremost interest in life is his family. The Linkletters have five children. They also have a family line they use when any member—including Art and his wife—starts complaining or recounting woes. This is how Art tells the true story of their well-used sentence. He said:

"Back in the days when we had only one child, who suddenly started a nosebleed, we were frantic. While I was trying to locate a doctor, my wife tried every home remedy she could think of: wet compresses, ice, a key down the back . . . I tell you, it was pandemonium.

"By the time our fifth child, Richard, came along, we were used to childhood emergencies. I was sitting in the living room when Richard rushed in with a pouring nosebleed. I took one look at our new wall-to-wall carpeting and yelled, 'Don't bleed in here!'"

Carol Lawrence and her husband Robert Goulet have a three-word phrase that has stopped many a small argument before it gets started. For instance, if Carol is still dawdling and Robert complains "For heaven's sake, we're a half hour late already!" Carol gives the three-word answer and Robert can't help but grin. The phrase came from a true happening and here is how Robert tells the story.

"While I was riding in a taxi, on my way to a restaurant, I noticed that the cab driver kept studying me in the mirror. Finally he said, 'You look like someone I know. Are you an actor?'

"I said I was and he asked, 'On television?'

"I said, 'Yes, I've been on television' and he asked, 'What's your name?' I just smiled.

"He said, 'Listen, Mister, if I go home and tell my wife that I had an actor in the cab and I don't know who he was she'll murder me.'

"As he was talking, we arrived at the restaurant. I found I only had a ten dollar bill and I handed it to him. He said, 'Now look Mister, you take a fifty cent ride, you gimme a ten dollar bill and you won't even tell me your name . . . Are you the guy who married the Kennedy girl?'

" 'No, I'm not Peter Lawford,' I answered, getting out of the cab.

" 'Is your name O'Brian?' I shook my head. He said, 'Well, I ain't gonna change this bill until you tell me.'

" 'Alright,' I said, 'you win. I'm Robert Goulet.'

"He stared at me, then kept glancing at me suspiciously as he counted out my change. As I was entering the restaurant he yelled after me, happily, '*Hey, you're right!*' "

From Sam Levenson

Sam Levenson's own laughter rounds out the w's, dots the i's and crosses the t's of his wit and humor. It is infectious and audiences respond with delight.

His first taste of show business was in '40 when he and a group of fellow school teachers formed a band and got a summer job in the Catskills. Sam learned how to deliver stories and after six years of part-time engagements he could see that acting paid well. He took a leave of absence to try it out. By the time television took hold, he had perfected his style of comedy and was an immediate hit as a guest on top variety shows. He soon had a sponsor and his own program.

The Levensons have a son and a daughter and in their household, when Sam leaves to keep a performing date, no one says "Good luck" or "Have a good show." Instead, they use the line from this true story that Sam tells.

"When our son Conrad was about three years old, he began to wonder why I left the house almost every night just as he was going to bed. One night, all dressed up in black tie, I came in to say good-night and he asked, 'Where are you going?'

" 'I'm going to work.'

" 'What do you do?'

" 'Well, I talk and the people laugh.'

"His lower lip began to quiver and on the verge of tears he sobbed, *I don't want anybody to laugh at my Daddy!*' "

Willie Mays was playing with semi-professional ball teams when he was only fourteen years old. He says he can't remember when he didn't know the game and added, "I'd play ball even if they charged me!"

The Giant scouts were so bowled over by Willie's ability that they bought his contract when he was fresh out of high school. Manager Leo Durocher, not usually given to such modesty, said, "God gave Willie the instincts of a ball player. All I had to do was to add a little practical advice about wearing his pants higher to give the pitchers a smaller strike zone. . . Hell, I learn about baseball just watching the kid!"

In person, Willie Mays has the "Say Hey" popularity that inspired the "Say Hey, Willie" song about him. He also has a salty sense of humor as you will see in this Mays family line, told by Willie.

"When I'm urged to go somewhere and I'm not in the mood, I often say, 'Go for me, too.'

"That line comes from the story about Pearl and Mabel. They were at a bar on their fourth drink when Pearl rose unsteadily and said, 'S'cuse me—I gotta go.' Mabel answered, 'As long as you're going, go for me, too.' Pearl said, 'O.K.' and out she went.

"When Pearl returned and caught sight of Mabel, she said in dismay, 'Ooo, I forgot to go for you! . . .' Mabel was indignant: 'You're a fine one! . . .' Pearl apologized, 'I'm sorry—I'll go for you now' and out she went for the second time.

"She returned a minute later and complained, 'You're a fine one—you didn't have to go at all!' "

Skitch Henderson was born in Birmingham, England, but he was transplanted early and grew American roots that spread into a whole television network. He has been a favorite TV character since '50 and his face is well-known to viewers, with and without his impish reddish-blonde beard. He is an accomplished pianist, composer, conductor, musical arranger—and is also quick at repartee. In short, he's a mighty handy man to have around a TV show.

In private life, Skitch is an avid aviation enthusiast and holds both a commercial pilot's and a soaring license. He is also an active member of the Automobile Racing Association and used to participate as a racing driver when he was a bit younger and a lot more carefree.

Everyone connected with a TV program knows that emergencies crop up frequently. When a frantic moment comes along, Skitch has a calming remark that came from a true happening. Here is how he tells about it.

"Andre Previn had been invited to come on *The Tonight Show.* He is an easygoing artist but his manager and his agent were worriers and each made a separate point of explaining how important it was to have the piano in perfect condition.

"Our piano is always in good shape but we called in two men to do a special job of cleaning, tuning and voicing the instrument. Thirty seconds before air time, someone brought in a soft drink and accidently pushed it over, spilling the entire contents into the piano.

"Andre looked at me aghast—his manager and agent, standing nearby, were horror stricken. I gave a sickly grin and offered the solution: '*Just give it the watered-down version!*'"

From Patrice Munsel

Patrice Munsel, the youngest singer to ever win a star contract from the Metropolitan Opera Company, is a rare combination. She has a rich, beautifully ranged voice, she can turn cartwheels and do a split, her face is a photographer's dream and her torso is even more so! She is married to Robert Schuler, a tall, handsome, successful businessman and they live with their four children in a whitewashed brick house in Long Island. Here is Patrice's favorite family saying.

"In our family, a compliment usually brings the answer 'You should have seen me last night.' Before you read the origin of this remark, I must explain that the movie star I am mentioning wasn't joking—she was absolutely serious.

"Bob and I were invited to dine at the home of a big Hollywood producer. As we sat down, our host turned to his guest of honor, a glamorous movie star, and said, 'My dear, you look absolutely radiant—you look incredibly lovely!'

"She turned slowly toward him, never batting an eyelash and answered, 'Thanks, sweetie, but did you see me at the premiere last night? I was more beautiful than I have ever been before in my whole life. I was fabulous. *You should have seen me last night!*' "

From Gypsy Rose Lee

The first time we met Gypsy Rose Lee was at a TV rehearsal. She sat patiently, crocheting a bedspread, while waiting to be called.

She's an author, a good photographer, an excellent cook, astute in business and a talented artist. Yet she is still most fondly known for her career of the 30's, when she was Queen of the Strippers, the royal monarch of the burlesque runway. It was while she was tantalizingly removing her garments at the first New York World's Fair, that Walter Winchell asked her to write a guest column. She found it fun and then wrote a best seller, *The G-String Murders*. A play followed, another book and then her autobiography *Gypsy* which became a hit Broadway musical.

Gypsy says, "As a kid I was called 'Plug.' I was too tall, too fat, I had a square Dutch bob and front teeth that pointed toward each other. My sister, June (Havoc), was the beauty and I was resigned to it." But Gypsy's mother, Rose, was never resigned to anything. Rose groomed her daughters for show business and was their producer, director, commanding officer and suspicious guardian. It was Rose's characteristic mistrust of human nature that gave her daughters this family line as told by Gypsy.

"Once, when I thought Rose had been too insulting to a very kindly, courteous theatrical agent, I chided her, 'Mother, don't you trust anyone?' She snapped, *'Trust in God but get it in writing!'* "

From Rudy Vallee

Rudy Vallee should have an honorary degree as a press agent from University of Maine where he spent his freshman year and from Yale, where he graduated. When Rudy crooned Maine's "Stein Song" and Yale's "Whiffenpoof," they became as well-known as his "My Time Is Your Time." Mr. Vallee doesn't like to be called "durable" but what better description is there for a man who started broadcasting in '28; had a national radio show for twenty years and then was a hit as a straight actor when *How To Succeed In Business Without Really Trying* opened on Broadway in 1961!

During his radio years, he also appeared in theaters, nightclubs, vaudeville, films and he wrote songs—of which the best known was "I'm Just A Vagabond Lover." Rudy and his crooning, his saxophone and his megaphone were familiar throughout the country. But, he does have a private life, including an exceptionally pretty wife, who inspired a family remark. Rudy said:

"This comment comes from my lovely bride who always tries to say something nice about everybody. We use it now when anyone is a nuisance or just plain nasty— *'He's not too bad looking for a homely man!'"*

Cheers And Jeers

Being only five feet tall, I have a limited capacity for anything alcoholic. If Arthur thinks I need a warning he says, *"Careful there, Mrs. Rappaport!"* This came from the time we were vacationing in a quiet Caribbean resort where most people were early to rise and early to bed. But, one Saturday night there was a long lasting cocktail party.

I was seated next to a very silent Englishman and I was having a tough time finding a topic for mutual conversation. I had tried books, sports, travel and the weather but heard only monosyllabic answers. I kept on talking. I also kept on sipping from a glass that our host repeatedly refilled. I must have finally hit on a subject to discuss, for during a lull in the general chatter, Arthur and everyone else heard me assuring my companion . . . "You're absolutely right. I am in complete rappaport!"

A writer once asked Ray Bolger why he became a dancer and he said, "I was a wallflower in high school and I heard a girl say, 'No matter what the band plays, Ray does the waltz!' So I decided to show her!'"

He started learning from the school night watchman, an ex-hoofer, and next, from a ballet teacher who exchanged lessons for bookkeeping. By then he was hooked on show business and did vaudeville turns in tank towns. He followed that with an uphill climb on Broadway and reached stardom in '36 with *On Your Toes*. After that, all Ray Bolger shows were hits, including *Where's Charlie?* which he later repeated as a movie and had the whole nation singing "Once In Love With Amy."

Ray married Gwen Rickard, a song writer, in '29. She was so devoted to his career that he said, "Gwen does everything for me but dance."

Here is a Bolger line, told by Ray.

"When I disagree and someone tries to pin me down to my reason, I often give this ungrammatical answer, '*It don't appeal to me.*'

"This came from the story about Becky who found herself in trouble and went to a shady doctor. The fee was set and then the doctor asked, out of curiosity, 'Who's the man?' Becky answered, 'Semmy Cohen.'

"Six months later she was back again, on the same errand. The doctor again asked, 'Who's the man?' and Becky again answered, 'Semmy Cohen.'

"When she came back for the third time, in the same fix, the doctor said, 'Now don't tell me it's that same fellow again!' Becky nodded. The doctor demanded: 'Why don't you marry the guy?' Becky shrugged—'*He don't appeal to me.*'"

From Leonard Lyons

Leonard Lyons has covered Broadway and café society fronts for his syndicated column since '34 but he's as eager and bright-eyed as when he started. He's thin, wiry, energetic and his writing, too, has snap and sparkle.

When Leonard enters a night spot—and his beat includes them all—he can "case the joint" faster than a cop. He may stop and chat briefly with a dozen or more people and most of them have a story or item to tell him. He'll grin and say "That's great" but it's only when the little black notebook and pencil come out that you know the item will be in.

Sylvia and Leonard were married the year he became a columnist and they have four sons. They all like traveling but Sylvia is a gypsy—she'll leave at the drop of a toothbrush. The Lyons have a family line that came from one of Sylvia's impulsive trips. It's their way of saying, "Enjoy yourself—it's later than you think."

Sylvia was having dinner with the Albert Laskers who were flying to California that night for a party-of-the-year to be given by Frank Loesser. The Laskers urged Sylvia to come along and she did but by the time they reached a stopover in Chicago, she felt remorseful and telephoned Leonard. "Come on out and join us," she coaxed, "it will be a wonderful party." Leonard was aghast. "What, fly all the way out to California for a party!" Sylvia answered, *"If it was for a funeral you'd fly!"*

From Victor Borge

Victor Borge is a Dane by birth but a dean of American show business, with a huge and devoted following of TV viewers and theatergoers. Like all well-known stars, Mr. Borge is frequently greeted by people who are not even vaguely familiar to him. If his wife, Saana, is along and asks him, "Who are they?" he answers as his son did in this true incident.

The Borges have five children and when their youngest boy was four years old he was invited to a swimming pool birthday party. When the little boy returned, his father asked him, "Did you have a good time?"

" 'Yes, father.'

" 'Did you have ice cream and cake?'

" 'Yes, father.'

" 'Were there lots of boys and girls in swimming?'

" 'Yes, father.'

" 'Were there more boys than girls in the pool?'

" *'I don't know. They didn't have clothes on.'* "

From Mike Douglas

Mike Douglas, whose phenomenally successful TV show is seen in all major cities, is what is known in the trade as a sweet guy. He is amiable, gracious and has a charming personality that reaches right through the television screen.

The Douglases have three daughters and Mike said, "My wife and I learned long ago that your own children's bright sayings should be enjoyed at home. We have a family comment we make when a proud parent or grandparent monopolizes the conversation.

"It comes from the time that our show was broadcasted from Cleveland. As I left the studio one day, a woman who was holding a little girl by the hand stopped me. She not only stopped me—she grabbed my arm. She said:

" 'Mr. Douglas, I think my little girl should be on your show.' Then she turned to the child, 'Charmine, dance for Mr. Douglas!' Charmine went into a tap routine while I stood there, trapped. As the child finished, her mother demanded, 'What do you think of her? . . .' I said, weakly, 'She's very cute—very talented—very nice little girl.'

"The mother said, 'You bet she is—and she's pretty, too, isn't she?' I nodded. 'Indeed she is. . . .' 'Isn't she one of the prettiest little girls you've ever seen?' I nodded again.

"The mother said, 'If you think she's pretty when you look at her—*you should see her pictures!* '"

Back in the summer of '38, the Herb Caen column burst into print in San Francisco. Within a few weeks of enjoying Caen's breezy, witty items, the average newspaper reader would scan the front page and then quickly turn to "see what Herb had to say."

Mr. Caen's style of humor is now widely known through the syndication of his column and through his six books, all devoted to the captivating enchantment of San Francisco. His newest book is being done in collaboration with the well-known artist, Dong Kingman.

Now for the Caen family line. If you have a spouse of middle years, who starts cutting up in youthful fashion, you'll have use for this line yourself. Here is how Herb tells it:

"After a black tie party, my wife talked me into going to a Rock 'n' Roll joint. Well, between the music and the drinks I finally agreed to go on the dance floor with her even though I was at least thirty years older than anybody in the place.

"For a full set of music I threw myself into what seemed to me a quite creditable imitation of what the young dancers around me were doing . . . the current Frug, Watusi, Monkey and Jerk.

"I felt pretty good as we walked off the dance floor until we passed a table of four teen-agers who apparently had been watching me in awe and disbelief. There was no comment as my wife walked by but as I tottered along in my dinner jacket, mopping my brow, one of the boys looked at me and said, softly, with infinite compassion, 'Well, *Voh-DOH-de-oh-DOH!*'"

From Herbert Mayes

Editor Herbert Mayes is a brilliant, tireless perfectionist. Grace Mayes was once asked, "How many hours a day does your husband work?" She answered, "He has cut down lately. He's only working a half day—12 hours."

Mr. Mayes started as editor of trade publications and then became editor of *Pictorial Review*. After that, he edited *Good Housekeeping*. During those years he wrote *Alger, A Biography Without A Hero*. He also compiled a volume of short stories, *Editor's Choice*. This was a collection of his favorites among the stories he had selected for *Good Housekeeping*. Studying Mr. Mayes' preface and the examples that follow is a postgraduate course in short story writing. But, Mr. Mayes found the greatest scope for his ability when he became editor of *McCall's* in '59, and elevated that magazine into the top leadership of its field. The shining proof of his discerning and critical judgment was found on every page—from cover through art work, fiction and features.

Mr. and Mrs. Mayes and their daughters, Victoria and Alexandra, have a line that is a family standby whenever the wisdom of some decision is questioned. It answers "What on earth ever made you do that?" and it comes from this story told by Mr. Mayes.

"In ancient days, a king sentenced a man to die. The man pleaded for a reprieve, promising to teach the king's horse to fly within one year. The king granted the request but warned the man that he would certainly be put to death at the end of the year if his pledge was not fulfilled. Friends came and asked, 'How could you make so rash a promise?' The man replied, 'Within a year the king may die, or I may die, or the horse may die. Besides, *in a year the horse may learn to fly.*'"

From Orson Bean

If you heard Orson Bean on Ed Sullivan's or other TV shows, you know he is a great talker. Yet, he is a second cousin of the late President Coolidge.

When Orson was a little boy named Dallas Burrows, living in Cambridge, Massachusetts, he received a magic set for his eighth birthday. He never recovered, and, later became an amateur magician in Boston. Next stop was the Blue Angel, in New York, where he was hailed as a refreshing discovery. By then, he had developed an amusing patter that worked better than magic. His Broadway debut followed and Mr. Bean has been kept busy ever since. One of his long runs was in *Will Success Spoil Rock Hunter?* in which he played opposite Jayne Mansfield. "That," he says, "accounts for my bad posture."

The Beans live in picturesque old Macdougal Alley, Greenwich Village, with their small daughter. This is one of their family sayings, as told by Orson.

"Whenever my wife ·Carolyn and I are trapped at a terrible show or a boring party, we look at each other and mumble *'The tide went out.'*

"This comes from a wonderful gag told by Fred Allen about spending his summers in a little town on the coast of Maine. Then he added, 'This town was so dull that one day the tide went out and never came back!' "

From Cleveland Amory

Cleveland Amory's *Proper Bostonians* is a sage, sassy history of Boston society from colonial times on. When the First Families read it they shuddered and skeletons rattled. If it is true that in Boston, the home of the cod, "the Lowells talk to the Cabots and the Cabots talk only to God," Mr. Amory knows what they say. He could write the book with authority for his family had long been of the upper upper class and he was well acquainted with fact and legend. Mr. Amory was also well equipped to write—he had spent most of his college years working on the *Harvard Crimson* and afterward, had been a reporter and editor. In fact, he was the youngest editor ever hired by the *Saturday Evening Post*.

Other society scene books followed, each written with accuracy and impudence—*Home Town, The Last Resorts, Who Killed Society.* Latest is his encyclopedic *Celebrity Register*, done with publicist Earl Blackwell. Mr. Amory's articles appear in national magazines, in his syndicated newspaper column and he is seen on TV as a commentator and panel guest. Though Mr. Amory lives in New York with his wife and their daughter, his story shows that he is still, properly, a Bostonian.

"I have always endeavored to instill my family with liberal doses of Boston homilies—'wear it out,' 'eat it up,' 'make-do,' 'do without,' etc. Now and then, however, my New York-born wife hears one too many and on one occasion, she took me to task.

"She said, 'You know, you're always talking about Boston but I notice that your father didn't marry a Bostonian, your brother didn't marry a Bostonian, your sister didn't marry a Bostonian and *you* didn't marry a Bostonian! . . .' I gave her my best long-suffering look—'We can't,' I explained, *'we have to spread the culture.'* "

From *Shari Lewis*

Imagine—pretty Shari Lewis was once just an offstage noise! Fresh out of Music and Art High School she studied ventriloquism while laid up with a broken ankle. She became so adept that she was hired as the "voice" for chickens, cats, dogs and even airplanes. But, she had a background of training in violin, piano, voice, drama, ballet and puppetry and she was still a youngster when she was writing her own music and material for her daily TV puppet show. Emmy and Peabody Awards followed; so did her popular recordings and books.

Shari is married to Jeremy Tarcher, a TV producer, and they have a little girl. They also have this family line, as Shari tells it.

"When utter confusion sets in, we have one word for it—'Garbage.' This is how it started. We have a sailboat and one blissful week we anchored north on the Hudson River as we peacefully rocked and read.

"At the end of the week, all was well except that we had a huge bag of rubbish. We started toward the next boat basin to drop it off but the wind and the current were so strong that we couldn't land. A man standing on the dock called, 'Can I help you?' Jeremy said, 'Throw him the bag.' I said, 'Oh, we can't do that!' 'Don't be silly,' he said, 'THROW IT!'

"So I picked up the bag and heaved it just as the man yelled, 'What is it? . . .' The bag hit him full force, broke, and the stuff spilled all over him as I yelled back, '*Garbage!*' "

Hugh O'Brian has been described as rugged, dashing and handsome. But in the television industry he is described as "a good property" because it pays to have him under contract.

As Wyatt Earp, Hugh had a huge following of men viewers but that is taken for granted when a good actor appears in Westerns. What sent Hugh's ratings sky-high is that he also had a huge number of women viewers—well proven when a sponsor sold tons of shampoo through the *Wyatt Earp* shows.

Hugh was born in Rochester, New York; joined the Marines when he was eighteen and became the youngest drill instructor in the history of the Corps. He has leadership qualities in business, too, and cashed in with merchandise labeled "Wyatt Earp"—clothing, badges, comic books, etc.

Part of Hugh's romantic appeal is that he is still a bachelor. But he and his friends have a "line" and here is how he tells it.

"We have our own way of saying, 'That's a pretty good guess.' It comes from the time that a large sized woman, wearing tight slacks and sweater, was imbibing freely in a crowded downtown bar.

"She struggled to her feet, cupped her hands together as though holding something in them and yelled for attention. She announced: 'Anybody who can guess what I got in my two hands can go home with me!'

"A man's voice called from the rear: 'Is it a five-hundred pound canary? . . .' She peered into her cupped hands and answered joyfully, *'Tha'sh close enough!'* "

From Jerome Beatty, Jr.

Jerome Beatty, Jr. writes a merry, witty column called "Trade Winds" for the *Saturday Review*. He is also the author of five very successful children's books and both hard-cover and paperback books for adults.

Jerry and his wife Joann live in a house on the water off Cape Cod, where she paints, while he writes. They have four daughters who were evidently spaced to avoid a population explosion—for, at one time, the youngest was in kindergarten while the oldest was in college. Here is one of the Beatty family lines as Jerry tells it . . .

"I originally heard this story from Paul B. Lowney and I like to use the tag line when I bring out refilled glasses for guests who are visiting us.

"Two men went into a restaurant. One of them said to his waiter, 'I want a glass of tea, very weak, with a piece of lemon.' The other said, 'I want a glass of tea, strong, no lemon, but be sure the glass is clean.'

"The waiter wrote it all down. He returned in a few minutes with the order and said, 'Now, *which one gets the clean glass?*' "

From Bob Cummings

Everyone who watches Bob Cummings in a movie or on television notices his remarkably youthful, virile aura of good health. But not everyone knows the background of that product of physical culture. Bob's mother was a minister of the Gospel, his father was a doctor and both parents believed in sound, sensible diet. They held militant guard over little Bob—no candy, no pastry, cake, cookies or tarts, no ice cream or sweets of any kind. So if you envy Bob Cummings' clear eyes, unblemished skin and perfect teeth, remember his underprivileged childhood!

Bob and his wife have seven children and they've tried to follow the diet doctrine that worked so well with Bob. There have been many slip-ups. But, when a Cummings child goes to a birthday party, he knows he can bring home his untouched candy basket and uneaten slice of cake and turn in those goodies for cash. With seven children, a household has disruptions. But Bob claims that one little phrase has calmed many a storm. Here is his message . . .

"When our daughter Melinda was a toddler, she was being enormously frustrated by her big brother Robert. He kept teasing her and holding her favorite toy just out of reach. Small Melinda fussed, fumed and finally exploded with the line that we all use—'Robert,' she howled, *'you're being inspimple!'* "

From Mrs. Jack Paar

Jack Paar once said, "I like to think of myself not as a comic but as a humorist. To me, a comic says funny things. A humorist thinks funny things."

As a boy, Jack had to think more than talk because he stuttered. He is supposed to have cured himself by putting buttons in his mouth and reading aloud. Cured he is, with an awesome ability for entertaining as he talks on and on, ad-libbing as he goes. A favorite comment in the Paar family was explained by Jack's wife. Miriam. She said:

"Although Jack has been in broadcasting for many years, he has never been particularly enamored of performing.

"Not long ago our daughter Randy found a cartoon which seemed to sum up her father's feelings. The caption under the drawing has become our handiest family line for Jack's many emergency problems.

"The sketch showed two aerialists going through their act on a high trapeze. One unfortunate partner missed the other and was plummeting toward the ground as a bystander calmly observed: *'Oh well, that's show business.'* "

Dina Merrill had two strikes against her when she started out to be an actress—family and fortune. No one believed that the daughter of tremendously wealthy, socially established parents would ever have drive enough to work seriously and wholeheartedly.

Dina, who was christened Nedenia, is the daughter of Edward Hutton and tall, stunning Marjorie Merriweather Post-Close-Hutton-Davies-May. Dina's grandfather, C. W. Post, inherited about $100 million. The Huttons, including Dina's cousin Barbara, never counted their old money. They just buried it.

When Dina enrolled at the American Academy of Dramatic Arts she studied hard. She weathered the rigors of summer stock and did small parts on Broadway and TV before starting in films. In the movies, the combination of her classic beauty and dramatic ability made terrific impact.

Dina Merrill was married to Stanley M. Rumbough, Jr., who had been a Marine Corps flyer but well able to support a wife since he is one of the heirs to the Colgate estate. However, Dina was already an actress when he met her and during their marriage he never interfered with her career.

At home, Dina's interests are centered on her children. In that household, too, there are family sayings and here is how Dina explains one of their favorites.

"One common drawback of family life is that someone is always interrupting. We have a remark we use at such moments that came from my third child, Nina.

"Nina was about three years old at that time and just learning to say her prayers. She mumbled and I said, 'I can't hear you.' She turned and looked at me solemnly and answered, '*I wasn't talking to you!*'"

From Mrs. David Sarnoff

Lizette Sarnoff has a many faceted life and shines in each. As the wife of General David Sarnoff, she has been hostess to, and entertained by royalty. Her philanthropy is not limited to sizable donations . . . she has been a conscientious volunteer executive at the New York Infirmary for many years. She has keen, discriminating appreciation for all creative arts and, in later life, became a student at the Sculpture Center in New York, with skillful and admirable results. The Sarnoffs live in a large, handsome private house in midtown Manhattan, but the high ceilings and paneled walls have a surprisingly friendly atmosphere—all due to Lizette's warm personality.

We asked Mrs. Sarnoff for a family line. She thought for a few minutes, then smiled and asked, "Haven't you found that married couples acquire a bad habit of repeating the same thing to each other too often? . . . It can become very boring but we have a line that stops needless repetition.

"It comes from the old days when David was always preoccupied with professional problems. I understood—but still, a household has routine, too. Sometimes meals must take place on time, especially when there are commitments for the following hours.

"Whenever David was urged to come to the dinner table before he was good and ready, he used to make exactly the same answer, 'No soup has to be eaten as hot as it is served.'

"I must admit I got tired of that answer. So, one night when we were very late indeed, I said, 'Come dear, we must have dinner now.' As he started his usual answer, I chimed in with an imitation of his voice and made it a duet.

"Since then the words 'No soup' have become our family way of saying 'I heard that already.'"

From Guy Lombardo

It was in '27 when Guy Lombardo and his Royal Canadians had their first network radio show and he has been known ever since for playing "The sweetest music this side of heaven."

Guy was born in London, Ontario, Canada, and the whole family loved music and each other. They have always stayed together because they enjoy family life. At one time when there were fifteen Royal Canadians, five were Lombardos! A band member said, "It's not true that you have to be a relative to work here—but it helps!"

When a writer called the Lombardo music "corn," Guy said, "I play for people in love, not acrobats!" That may be the reason why Guy is still going strong as a top name on the popularity list.

Guy and his wife Lilliebell were married in '26. They both like speedboats and Guy is a skilled racer. They also like living at the seashore, which is where they acquired this family saying described by Guy.

"In our family, the comment '*You know what?*' means that you're about to leave the room. We were sitting on the beach at East Hampton watching two little boys who were playing on an overturned flat-bottom rowboat. They were about four or five years old and they were so skinny that their bathing trunks hung low on their hips.

"One little boy was evidently the leader. He piped out in a loud, shrill voice: 'I'm the Admiral! Ready— MARCH!' He and his friend then marched importantly around and around the boat. He gave further orders: 'Drop the anchor!' 'Board the ship!' Each command was followed by action.

"Suddenly the little Admiral stopped short and in his natural tone of voice said: 'You know what?' His friend asked, 'What?' . . . 'I gotta go to the bathroom.'"

From Ernest Borgnine

When Ernest Borgnine went to Hollywood, an agent tried to get him an audition. The casting director looked at his photos and complained, "But this guy looks like a truck driver!" "Perfect casting," the agent murmured. . . . Mr. Borgnine had driven a truck before enrolling in the U.S. Navy. His acting career was started at a dramatic school, under the G. I. Bill of Rights.

While still new in films, he played "Fatso," the brutal sergeant in *From Here To Eternity*. His characterization was so superb that he would probably have been limited to villainous roles. But *Marty* came along—and for his endearing, heartwarming, gentle performance, he won the Academy Award for Best Actor.

Mr. Borgnine's grandfather was a financial advisor to King Victor Emmanuel but Ernest doesn't take after him. Like many actors, he leaves money matters to his manager. When some investment has paid off well, Ernest has a line he quotes—and here is his story about it.

"Two men, who had gone to school together, met years later. One of them had never even been able to add two-and-two in school but he had become very wealthy. The other man had been the brightest boy in class. Yet, now he was dead broke and he asked, 'How come that you're so successful with the kind of lousy marks you used to get in school?' 'Very simple,' the rich guy answered, 'I buy for a dollar and sell for five. *You just can't beat that four percent interest!*' "

From Mrs. Kermit Kraus

A liability in family conversation is the hashing and rehashing of some subject. It can get mighty tiresome. Mrs. Kermit Kraus, well-known in New York as the owner of hair salons called "Ila's," told us a good line for finishing off an endless discussion. This is her story:

"The president of a Sisterhood was conducting a meeting. She rapped for order; cleared her throat and said, 'Ladies—if you please! . . . Today we have serious matters for our attention. So, there will be no talk about fur coats . . . you have fur coats—I have fur coats . . . There will be no talk about diamonds . . . You have diamonds—I have diamonds . . . There will be no talk about grandchildren . . . you have grandchildren—I have grandchildren . . . And, there will be no talk about sex . . . *What was—WAS!*' "

From Jan Murray

Jan Murray was a bean pole sized teen-ager with a quick wit and memory for jokes. An owner of Leon and Eddie's happened to catch Jan's patter at a party and hired him for a one-night stand. It was just for laughs— the club usually presented only well-known performers. Jan was hired for laughs—but he got them. The sophisticated audience thought the skinny kid was just great. Later, he opened in vaudeville at Loew's State on Broadway. With television, Jan became a very busy performer. He has been a guest on every major variety program and host of his own shows—*Songs For Sale, Treasure, Charge Account*, etc. But, he had an eye on the future and gave up easy TV money to gain experience in stock company drama, farce and musical comedy.

Now Mr. Murray is in films and lives in Beverly Hills with his wife, Toni, a beautiful ex-show girl, and their four children. Here is a family story that Jan tells.

"If you finally give in to stop an argument, you can enjoy the last word anyway, with this line.

"On a cold winter night, Abie was snoring peacefully when Becky pushed him and complained, 'Abie, so close the window—it's cold outside.' He grunted, turned on his side and went back to sleep. She pushed again. 'Abie, so close the window—it's cold outside! . . .' Once more he nestled into the covers and went back to sleep.

"At the third push and the third command, he threw back the blankets, clumped out of bed and slammed the window shut. Then he marched back and demanded, '*So now it's warm outside?*' "

From The Fredric Marches

As a child, Frederick Bickel got pretty tired of puns on "pickle." So as an actor, he dropped a "k," borrowed from Grandfather Marcher and became Fredric March.

Arriving in New York from the University of Wisconsin, he took a bank job and while at work, had acute appendicitis. Though his agony was genuine, his dramatic imagination applauded the fine show and when he recovered he decided "Stage not Cage." In order to eat, he worked as a film extra while calling on agencies. After a few encouraging roles, he joined a stock company where Florence Eldridge, already acclaimed on Broadway, was the leading lady. They were married, toured for the Theater Guild and were in Los Angeles when talking pictures started. Actors with trained voices took over and Fredric March won Oscars and praise for years of widely varied star performances. Together, too, the Marches shone in films and in dramatic plays—among them *Long Day's Journey Into Night*, in which Miss Eldridge broke hearts with her portrayal of the dope-addicted mother. They are a famous theatrical couple but they have a quiet home life, with a daughter and son who gave them this family line, told by Miss Eldridge.

"We have a phrase we use when anyone becomes too long-winded. It started when our daughter was about nine years old and went to see a moving picture with some school friends. At dinner that evening she recounted the entire plot, frame by frame.

"As our eyes became glassy, her seven-year-old brother spoke up—*'Just tell us the details!'* "

The Murrays Have A Word For Floozies

For years Arthur and I have referred to floozies as "rejects." Here is how the word came into our family lives.

Back in the 30's, long before we retired from the dance school business, a man stopped in at our New York studio and asked for information about taking dancing lessons. The young lady who greeted him told him the cost of instruction and gave him a short demonstration of our method of teaching. She made a special point of explaining that our instructors were not only thoroughly and carefully trained but were also very nice, well-bred people.

"We have to be careful," she said, "A great many girls who apply as teachers are very good dancers but they are turned down because they are—er—you know—sort of fast." The man looked up. "What do you do about those girls?" "Oh, we just take their names and put them in the 'reject' file."

She went on to arrange the new student's first appointment and asked him, "Do you have any preference—a short or tall girl—a blonde or brunette?" "I'm not fussy," he answered, "couldn't I have one of your 'rejects'?"

When Arthur Marx was asked why he hadn't gone on the stage he said, "My father, Groucho, told me an actor has a lousy life. I didn't see why—he seemed to be living pretty well. But I took his advice."

Instead, Mr. Marx writes for actors—on TV, for *Mc-Hale's Navy, My Three Sons, The Real McCoys* . . . for films, as co-author of Bob Hope's *Global Affair, I'll Take Sweden* and *Eight On the Lam* . . . He also co-authored the Broadway comedy hit, *The Impossible Years.* In this, Alan King played the father of a teen-age daughter, Linda. Commenting on Linda's messy room, the Marx line went "I'd have thrown-up except she'd never have noticed it!"

Arthur Marx' first book, *The Ordeal of Willie Brown,* was about a tennis player. It was partially autobiographical—Arthur had won the National Freshman Intercollegiate tournament. He also beat Jack Kramer but he says, "My biggest claim to tennis fame was getting the mumps at Sea Bright." Another of his books was *Not As A Crocodile* and his best seller, *Life With Groucho,* which ran serially in the *Saturday Evening Post.* His other writings have been humorous articles for national magazines.

Arthur and his wife Lois have a line that has stopped many a family argument. This is how Arthur tells it.

"When I was about seven years old, I wanted a BB gun and I pestered and whined and begged. Finally Groucho became exasperated and yelled, 'You'll never have a BB gun while I'm head of this house! . . .' I answered, *'If I had a BB gun, you wouldn't be head of this house!'* "

From Lawrence Welk

Mr. Welk has a soap-and-water country boy charm and comes by it naturally. He was born on a South Dakota farm and didn't try his musical bent until he was twenty-one. He says, "My folks didn't approve of worldly ways." At voting age, Lawrence formed a novelty band and next, had a group he called The Hotsy Totsy Orchestra, a strange choice of name for a man who plays what Broadway labels as "Schmaltz." At that time he was broadcasting on radio but it was television that has made Lawrence Welk one of the best known, most popular and most successful band leaders.

The Welks have three children and live quietly and simply. If needed, Lawrence can be quite a handy man around the house and grounds. Busy with such jobs, his family like to remind him that he looks far different from his well-groomed television image. They use the remark from this story, told by Mr. Welk.

"One feature of our show that has special fascination for ladies in the studio audience is when a few of them cut-in to dance with me. I'd like to think it's my dancing ability they enjoy but I'm afraid they just want to be seen by the folks back home. Usually this spot goes smoothly but one day, I was 'tagged' with a vigorous whack on the back by a determined lady of generous proportions. 'I've never danced,' she told me, 'but I've come 3,000 miles to see this show and to dance with you!'

"She went into a pump-handle routine, obviously unaware that the man is supposed to lead. With the camera on us, I tried to get into the very basic 'a-one-and-a-two' that I use for such emergencies. It was hopeless—I had finally tangled with an immovable object.

"The topper came when the lady gave me a withering stare and said, '*Mr. Welk, on television you look like a much better dancer!*'"

From Groucho Marx

It would be a nice twist to be able to say that Groucho Marx, in private life, is gentle and shy. He is about as gentle as a shark and as shy as a barracuda!

Mr. Marx is an exceptionally well-informed man and he has no patience whatsoever with adult dullards. His only soft, sentimental side is reserved for children. With them, a metamorphosis sets in and he becomes tender, tolerant and simply charming. His books, *Many Happy Returns* and *Groucho and Me* are clever, amusing and sharp. If he wrote for children, he could weave magic.

Groucho has some wonderful stories about his father, Sam. One anecdote ends with a line that has become a family answer when anyone says, "I'll bet you I'm right!" Here is how Groucho told me the story.

"Sam was in the audience watching us perform. During the intermission, he heard the man in back of him say, 'They're not brothers. I know they're not—they don't even look alike.' Sam turned around and said, softly, '*I* think they're brothers.' The man snorted, 'And I say they're not brothers. I'll bet you five bucks!'

"Sam considered carefully and then answered, '*What odds will you give me?*'"

From Bert Parks

Undoubtedly, there is no M. C. more handsome nor virile than Bert Parks. Men liked his rapid fire delivery on TV's *Break The Bank, Stop The Music, Double Or Nothing*—but the ladies adored him. Bert once ruefully called himself "the darling of the menopause set." He still M.C.'s the gigantic *Miss America Pageant* but he has also become a popular actor, starring in *Music Man* on Broadway and taking the show on tour.

Annette and Bert Parks, their twin sons and daughter, have a close family relationship. They also share a phrase that they use when they don't want to be dragged into an argument. Here is how Bert tells the background story.

"A married couple had a house guest who stayed on and on. He was the wife's brother and early one morning the husband whispered to her, 'How long is that brother of yours going to stay?' 'I don't know,' she whispered back. Her husband said, 'I'll tell you what we'll do. We'll pick a fight and whoever he says is wrong will throw him out—O.K.?' She agreed.

"They went down to breakfast where their guest was eating—as usual. They fought, as planned, and at the height of the argument, the husband turned to his brother-in-law and demanded, 'So who is right—is she right or am I?' The guy kept on eating and answered, '*I don't know from nothing—I'm staying two more weeks.*'"

From Mrs. Herman Schoenberg

Mrs. Herman Schoenberg is married to a well-known New York surgeon. She likes to travel and entertain; she does social service work and she tells her husband what to take for a cold. Here is the story that Mrs. Schoenberg told us:

"Herman and I have a phrase we use when anyone comments on a couple who seem oddly matched. It's our way of answering the question: 'What did *he* see in her?'

"It comes from the time that a friend of mine told us some wonderful news. Her father-in-law, who had been a widower and very lonely, was going to be married again. Pop was seventy-eight but the bride-to-be was charming, congenial and of suitable age. The whole family was delighted and they were planning a big wedding and reception.

"The wedding took place and the next morning my friend was a little worried about the newlyweds. After all, it had been a long, exciting and tiring evening. But she hesitated about phoning—after all, what could she say to a bridegroom of seventy-eight the day after the wedding?

"Finally she did call and her father-in-law answered. She took a deep breath and said, brightly, 'Hello, Pop. How is everything?'

"Pop's voice was strong and hearty and he boomed out: 'Everything's fine! She's wonderful—she's marvelous —*can she cook oatmeal!*' "

From Ozzie Nelson

Say "Ozzie" to almost anyone in the U.S.A. and he'll add "Nelson," for Ozzie Nelson has become an American institution, with a background almost too good to be true. During college he played star football, was a welterweight champ, varsity swimmer, president of the Student Council, art editor of the magazine—all while working his way through by running a dance band.

Ozzie came out with a law degree but he preferred music and by '33 his band was on prime radio time. He hired a pretty vocalist, Harriet Hilliard, and they were married two years later. They blended smoothly on radio and in films and when *The Adventures of Ozzie and Harriet* moved to TV in '51, they and their two sons, Rickey and David, were adored by viewers.

Before the boys were born, Ozzie and Harriet used to tour with the band and this family line, told by Ozzie, started then.

"Back in '41, we were in San Francisco before starting one-night stands through the Northwest. We hired an eighteen-year-old fellow named Angelo to take care of the car during the tour. He was a nice kid but he had one bad fault—he never took the blame for anything. It was one of Angelo's classic excuses that we all use when we goof.

"Angelo was to park the car and bring it to the stage door after each show. He was very careful and always locked the doors. Unfortunately he continually locked up, leaving the key in the ignition. Each time he had a different excuse but I finally said, 'Angelo, the next time this happens, you're going home!'

"For a week all went well. Then one night when we came out—no car. I went to the parking lot and found Angelo trying to unlock the car door with a wire coat hanger. I stood there glaring at him until he looked up and said, innocently, 'Oz, *you done it again!*' "

The late Billy Rose may have given the clue to his rather Napoleonic attitude when he said, "It's tough to be five three in a five nine world."

With childhood memories of sidewalk evictions for lack of rent and of being shrimp bait for tall bullies, it's not surprising that financial success turned him wary. He was hated, admired, feared and loved, too, despite himself.

He wrote some tremendous song hits; owned nightclubs; produced *Jumbo*—a circus musical that made a million; staged dazzling Aquacades; owned a theater with his name and a town house full of art treasures. None of this would instill modesty in a small-sized man with bitter memories.

With all Billy's faults, he had endearing qualities, including a sense of humor. When I was just starting this collection, I asked him for a "line" and he said, "Why don't you use the one that you and Arthur always kid me about? . . ." Here it is—the Billy Rose remark that Arthur and I use whenever anyone talks at length and no one else can get a word in.

It happened one night when Billy wandered into Sardi's restaurant alone, and came over to sit at our table. He told us about his new house in Montego Bay and fifteen minutes went by as he described it in detail. He went on to tell us about his recent investments and gave us his opinions on the stock market. He followed this by telling us about his newest acquisitions in art work. By now an hour had gone by, with Billy's voice the only one heard at our table.

He suddenly looked at his watch and said, "I've got to go. *Is there anything else you want to say to me?*"

To home viewers and to those in show business, Ed Sullivan is the King of Television. Making an appearance on an *Ed Sullivan Show* has enormous prestige plus the opportunity of performing before a fantastically large audience. So it would seem that after all these many years of popularity, Mr. Sullivan might well have become autocratic and dictatorial. He hasn't. He is unfailingly courteous and especially gentle to performers who are trembling with stage fright. One young singer told her agent: "Mr. Sullivan was so kind. He patted me on the shoulder and said, '*Win, lose or draw*, I think you're great!'" Mrs. Sullivan explained that these words come from a family saying. Here is the background story, just as tall, glamorous Sylvia Sullivan told it:

"Our 'secret' rallying cry of encouragement and affection has just four words but it is amazing the comfort it has given us—jointly or singly—whenever we have faced a crisis.

"Our code dates back to one tense morning when our distraught twelve-year-old daughter, Betty, was to take her first big school exam at Marymount. Propped on the breakfast table, leaning against her egg cup, Betty found a note from her Daddy:

'*Win, lose or draw*, we love you.'"

From My Brother Norman

My brother Norman was reading some of these family lines and he asked, "You're going to include Grandpa's favorite, aren't you?" Norman was right. Grandpa's line belongs here. It has always been used in our family by anyone who feels he has been treated unfairly. Here is the background story as Norman remembers it.

"A poor guy, ragged and down to his last dime, was sitting dejectedly on a park bench when a friend of his came along. 'You know,' he said to the friend, 'I've been sitting here and thinking how unfair this world is. The rich have all the good fortune and the poor have nothing but misfortune.' He went on. 'For the rich—a car. The poor must walk. For the rich—fine clothes. The poor wear rags. For the rich—thick steaks. The poor eat bread. . . .'

"In the midst of this recital of woe, a bird dropping fell on the poor guy's sleeve. 'You see? *For the rich they sing!*'"

From Henny Youngman

Henny Youngman tells jokes with the rapid fire delivery and the intonation of a Borscht Circuit comedian. But, he was born in London, England. He said:

"I was always a ham. Even when I was a little kid, I knew I was going to go in show business. My family had other ideas—and had me take lessons on the violin . . . To me, it was a fiddle and I made my start playing with a band.

"From there I got in with a comedy group. We did songs, musical numbers and made funny remarks. We played some very tough night spots. It wasn't easy the way it is now when I go on the Carson or Gleason shows or on *Hollywood Palace* . . . No, in those days you had to handle the smart alecks—the ones who tried to heckle. So you returned insult for insult—things like: 'When snakes get drunk, they see him! . . .' 'Look at him—sex takes a holiday! . . .' 'Madam—and I believe that is your right title!' "

The Youngmans and their son and daughter have a family comment that they automatically make to a bachelor. Henry tells it this way.

"Two fellows meet and one asks, 'How's your wife?' The other guy answers, 'I'm not married.' The first man asks, '*What do you do for aggravation?*' "

From Beatrice Lillie

Beatrice Lillie is undoubtedly the most beguiling, adored comedienne in England and America. Her sense of timing shows exquisite perfection in her pantomime and in her delivery of speech. But in private life, as Lady Peel, she delivered a "line" once too often! Here is her account of it. She said:

"Gossip is quite wrong, of course. It's a time killer—it's even shameful—but what is more titillating than a snippet of sex gossip?

"I always listen; hear the whole irresistible thing through and at the tail end, it's fun to fluff off the story with some throw-away comment. My pet remark used to be: '*Now, tell me, dear, were you under the bed?*'

"That little question became rather a standard saying of mine until one night in London when we were at a fancy party after the theater. A famous actress carried on with a report of a hot love affair and we all sat there, hooked, with our chins on our hands and our ears wide open. She didn't miss a trick. Every detail was vividly presented—how many times a week the lovers met; how they would get potted on Dom Perignon; the jillions of passion kisses—well, you know the rest.

"We were all fascinated and terribly impressed and there was awed silence at the end of the living, breathing drama. It was then that I archly asked, 'Now, tell me, darling, were you under the bed?' She heaved her bosom and answered, 'My dear, I was *in* it!'"

From Virginia Graham

Without Virginia Graham, her TV show, *Girl Talk*, would be babble. She stirs up fascinating controversies among the guests and brings out meows. She invites confessions, too . . . Ilka Chase, whose letter paper had been engraved "Mrs. Louis Calhern," sent the leftovers to his next wife. Guests are told to dress appropriately for morning hours. Zsa Zsa came in her usual style and Virginia asked, "What opera is opening?"

But there is much more to Virginia Graham than banter. She was a reporter while still in high school and, later wrote radio commercials before having her own shows reporting fashions, news, cooking. She claimed, "I have the perfect face for radio!"

Women love Virginia's remarks . . . on Jack Paar's Show she said, "I'm the one who looks like two June Allysons!" And this one: "I've been a blonde so long that my blood was typed 'C' for Clairol." Women also love to hear about Harry to whom Virginia has been blissfully wed since '35.

When Virigina is dressed in her best, her family enjoys asking a certain question. Here is how she explains their remark.

"Our tiny granddaughter, Jan, had always seen me well-groomed and nicely made-up—just as she sees me on television. Then came the day when I was just back from an exhausting ten day tour. I put on a terry robe, set my hair in rollers and covered my head with an old pink net cap that had a moth-eaten rose hanging from it like a drunken miner's lamp.

"The doorbell rang and in came our daughter Lynn, with little Jan along. They wanted to surprise me. Jan rushed over, hugged and kissed me and then stepped back and took a good look at me. She turned to her mother and asked, doubtfully, *'This is my Nana, isn't it?'*"

From Irving Mansfield

Irving Mansfield, producer of the popular TV program *Talent Scouts*, is married to glamorous Jacqueline Susann, author of *Every Night, Josephine* and the sizzling new best seller *Valley Of The Dolls*.

We were having dinner with the Mansfields when a curvy girl in a tight dress with a low, low neckline came over to our table. She stood directly opposite Irving, leaned over further than a Bunny, and said, "Mr. Mansfield, I'd do anything for a chance to get on your show. Won't YOU give me an audition yourself?"

Irving made a stab at politely rising, even though he was seated against the wall, and he tactfully explained that the booking agents for the show had to give all the auditions. He suggested that she write to the office.

As the girl left, Irving murmured something and he and Jackie grinned broadly. I asked, "What was that you just said?" Irving answered, "Oh, that's just a line of Jackie's that we often use at times like this. You see, when a show is on, we get a huge number of letters requesting auditions or interviews. Practically all of the mail goes to the office where it is handled by regular routine. But, now and then, some ambitious young 'hopeful' finds out our home address and writes to me there.

"Like all wives, Jackie has been known to read all the mail. One day she opened an envelope and out dropped a photo of a gorgeous girl in a bikini. The girl was well endowed and the bikini left very little to the imagination. She wrote that she was a singer and she added, 'Mr. Mansfield, I'd do ANYTHING to get on *Celebrity Talent Scouts*. And when I say ANYTHING—I mean ANYTHING!'

"So Jackie answered this letter. She sent the girl one of her own most flattering pictures and wrote, 'I am Mrs. Mansfield. And *I do EVERYTHING for Mr. Mansfield. And when I say EVERYTHING—I mean EVERYTHING!*'"

From David Janssen

David Janssen, TV star of *The Fugitive* series, started in films at the tender age of eight. Much later, after two years in the Army, he was cast—over and over—as what he calls an "agree-er." He explained, "The star would ask, 'Isn't that so?' I would agree, as the script required, and then disappear."

Despite such modesty, Mr. Janssen was noticed and was signed to star in the long-running TV series, *Richard Diamond*. He then had film roles in *Hell to Eternity, Man Trap, My Six Loves* and others. He also guest starred in TV dramas and says, "Sometimes I was the good guy—sometimes the bad—I just like to work steadily."

Mr. Janssen takes his handsome appearance lightly for he has always been surrounded by good looks. His mother was a "Miss Nebraska," one sister was a "Miss California" and his wife, Ellie, is tall and beautiful. He and Ellie live in a posh section of Beverly Hills and soon after they moved in, a friend phoned and asked, "David, is it raining out there?" He answered, "It wouldn't dare —not at these prices."

The Janssens have a family comment they make when anyone is absentminded. They say, *"They're shooting that at Warner's."* David explains.

"After being under contract at Universal for five years, appearing in thirty-two pictures, I was finally given a good part in *Lafayette Escadrille*. I was due on the set at 6:30 and left home about 5 A.M., driving in a half dreamy state. I walked into "Make-up" and the guy said, 'What are you doing here?' I answered, 'What do you think I'm doing! I'm here for *Escadrille*.' He said, 'I hate to shock you, but, they're shooting that at Warner's!'

". . . Like an old milk horse on its rounds, I had gone back to Universal."

If Dr. Joyce Brothers had reacted with normal feminine vanity, she would never have earned a quarter of a million dollars in three years.

Back in '55, Joyce was shampooing her blonde hair when the phone rang. "This is *The $64,000 Question.* We received your application and have just had a cancellation for tonight. Can you get here immediately? . . ." With soap in her eye, Joyce said, "I'll be there"; called a friend to take care of the baby, wrapped a towel around her head and ran to catch a cab.

When the idea of applying for the quiz show first occurred to her, Joyce decided that "Boxing" would be a good category. It didn't take her Doctorate in Psychology to figure out that a producer would like to have a woman as a prizefight expert. First she boned up thoroughly on the subject and then wrote in. Winning the quiz show led to TV guest appearances, to her own TV show and to her best selling book *Ten Days To A Successful Memory.*

Joyce is married to Dr. Milton Brothers (M.D.) and they live in Manhattan with their daughter Lisa who—as Joyce explains—started this family line.

"Milton and I have a phrase we use when anyone is looking for an excuse and tries to put the blame elsewhere. We had bought a Polaroid camera for our daughter's birthday and my husband showed her very carefully how to develop the pictures.

"Lisa was thrilled and posed our entire family group, including aunts, uncles and grandparents and then took her very first snapshot. She developed it, just as she was taught, took one look at the blurred results and wailed, *'Everybody moved!'* "

From Myron Cohen

Myron Cohen has appeared repeatedly during every year that Ed Sullivan has had a TV show. He has also been a frequent guest for Johnny Carson. And, year 'round, he is kept busy as a headliner in big time night-clubs. But, for twenty-five years before all this limelight, he used to sell dress fabrics to the wholesalers. Myron said, "I told stories in those days, too, but it was to break down buyer-resistance."

When he was a salesman, Myron and his wife, Miriam, used to go regularly to the Sunday *Celebrity Nights* at Leon and Eddie's, the site now occupied by Toots Shor's. Actors would drop in; be introduced and most of them did a few minutes of stand-up chatter. Myron explained: "People like Bob Hope, Joe E. Lewis, Jackie Gleason came there . . . Then one Sunday, Eddie Davis, who had been assured that I could tell stories, called on me. He introduced me as a professor of languages and I shook all the way to the stage. I managed to talk and, thank goodness, the audience laughed—among them was Lou Walters who owned the Latin Quarter. Lou phoned me the next day and asked how I'd like to be a replacement for nine days in Miami. He offered me $1,250 a week! I was overwhelmed—and scared to death. It turned out to be quite a thrill and then, quite a come-down to go back to selling fabrics. Six months later I was out of the 'rag' business and into show business."

Myron has a saying that his family always used when-ever anyone tried to drive too sharp a bargain. Here is how he explains the origin of the remark.

"A little girl walked into a bakery and complained, 'My Mama found a fly in your raisin bread! . . .' The baker said, 'So *bring back the fly and I'll give you a raisin!*'"

Mark Goodson is a big surf rider of the air waves. He and his partner, Bill Todman, started together in '46 and produced various radio game shows such as *Stop The Music, Hit the Jackpot, Rate Your Mate, Beat The Clock*. Then, in '49, their immortal baby was born—the TV panel program *What's My Line?* That, and the long list of television shows they have developed and produced make an awesome total. In the trade, it is said that they have an uncanny sense for choosing what the public wants.

Yet no matter how adroitly a show is planned and admired, it still has to be sold. There are times when a prospective sponsor praises but doesn't buy. He may say, "That's a great idea—that's terrific" . . . but then add, "Too bad we're not in the market right now or I'd sure grab that show." Compliments sound nice—a cash register sounds better. Mark Goodson has a favorite expression he uses around the office. It is based on a simple principle of merchandising and it comes from this story that he tells.

"A man walked into a delicatessen and asked, 'How much is your Swiss cheese?' The clerk answered, 'Two dollars a pound.' The customer was outraged and protested, 'Two dollars a pound! Why, that shop across the street is selling Swiss cheese for a dollar a pound.'

"The clerk shrugged. 'Then why didn't you buy it there?' and the customer said, 'They were out of it.' The clerk answered, *'When we're out of it we sell for fifty cents a pound.'* "

From Hy Gardner

Hy Gardner has had a humorous Broadway column since '34 and, as he says, "Before that, I tried to sell a column." His only intermission was when he served as a Captain in the AUS from '42 to '45.

He is the author of *Offbeat Guide to New York, Champagne Before Breakfast, So What Else Is New?* and *Tales Out Of Night School.* And, each week, he produces a New York TV show with a luminous list of guests including Maria Callas, Barry Goldwater, Maurice Chevalier, Groucho Marx—and Dempsey and Tunney together. Guests appear on Hy's show by invitation and no fee is paid. An interviewer once asked him, "How do you do it? All those big names—why, you even had Jack Benny for free!" Hy said, "It's easy. They know I'm going to let them do all the talking."

Hy's family line is one he and his wife both use whenever they want to avoid some entanglement. Here is how he tells it.

"Our remark stems from the story of a man who needed money desperately and telephoned a wealthy friend.

"He started with small talk . . . how are you; how is your family; how's your golf; when did you get back from abroad; are you using your yacht, etc. Finally, after some fifteen minutes of easy chatter, the caller got up his nerve and asked: 'Look, pal, I'm really up against it—will you lend me a hundred dollars?'

"There was a moment of complete silence at the other end of the wire and then a thinly disguised voice said, *'I'll tell him when he comes in.'*"

Marilyn used to be the right-hand gal in columnist Hy Gardner's office. Now she is Mrs. Gardner and the mother of their young son, Jeffrey. She is pert, pretty and smart and Hy gives her full credit for many ideas he has adopted. For example, the "Tip-off; Check-up" formula . . . these are items he runs in his column under that name. First he tells the tip-off rumor; then he gives the true check-up. They are often hilarious. Besides, it's fun to see behind a press agent's screen.

The Gardners live on the shoreline in Connecticut and commute to do a weekly TV show. Column and broadcast deadlines do not make for even-tempered tranquillity. But, when Hy blows his top about anyone, Marilyn can calm him down with the last line of this story. Here is how she tells it.

"An actor returned home late and found his wife lying on the floor, unconscious, battered and almost nude. He revived her and pleaded, 'Darling, what happened?'

"The wife howled, 'What happened? Why, that miserable agent of yours! He rang the bell, asked for you and when he found I was alone, he tried to make love to me. I fought him off—but he ripped my clothes, kissed me, hugged me and when I screamed, he knocked me unconscious. Then he splashed water on me to bring me to and repeated his attacks again and again, each time knocking me out cold when I screamed for help. That's all I remember.'

"The husband stared at her, then asked: *'Didn't he leave any message?'* "

From Cobey Black

Cobey Black is a leading feature writer on the *Honolulu Star-Bulletin*. She is a good-looking ex-actress, married to General Edward Black, and they have six youngsters. A mother of six develops a telepathic sense for spotting trouble. When one of her children acts overly innocent, Cobey grows suspicious and asks, "Were you playing on the roof? . . ." Her question comes from this story as she tells it.

"John and James were bachelor brothers, well past middle age. They lived with their elderly mother and the only friction in the household was that John had a pet cat, named Frisky, that James loathed. John had to go on a trip and he pleaded with his brother to look after his cat. James reluctantly agreed.

"When John returned, the first thing he asked was, 'How's Frisky?' 'Dead,' said James. John turned white and said, 'That's a shocking way to tell me!' James asked, 'What could I say?' and John told him, 'You could have broken the news gently . . . You could have said that Frisky was playing on the roof and that she lost her footing and fell and that the poor little thing was fatally injured. See what I mean?' 'I guess I do,' James said, 'I'm sorry.'

" 'We'll forget it,' John said, 'it's over . . . But, tell me, how is Mother?' James thought for a moment, then answered: 'Well, *she was playing on the roof. . . .*' "

Miss Havoc was known as Baby June when she started in vaudeville at two years of age. She was a dancing, singing wage-earner until the depression years of the early 30's. Then she took the only job she could get — in those grueling sessions of physical endurance called Dance Marathons. Reading about those days in her book *Early Havoc* and seeing them in her Broadway play *Marathon* makes your toes curl.

But she bounced up . . . and as an actress on Broadway, in motion pictures, and as an enchanting Titania of *Midsummer Night's Dream.* She toured Europe with the American Repertory Company and then visited thirty-two countries, co-starring in the State Department production of *Skin of Our Teeth.*

June lives in a doll-sized Connecticut house—so small that her sister Gypsy Rose Lee says you need a shoehorn to get in.

Miss Havoc has a line she uses for theatrical newcomers who take themselves too seriously. Here is how she explains the origin.

"Being raised on the circuit, I was cherished by hundreds of warmhearted vaudevillians. One old friend warned me of the dangers of vanity. He said, 'Don't show off, honey. Just remember the act that was on the way to Australia for a tenth-rate tour. He was a fellow who had always been a failure and was so unhappy that he threw himself over the rail into the sea . . . There was a lot of screaming and all the passengers lined the rail to watch rescue operations. Then the Captain hit him with the giant spotlight. Floundering in the water, he was so overjoyed by the sudden glory that he drowned himself taking bows! . . . So, honey, *don't be too proud too fast!*' "

From Bil Baird

Bil Baird, who designs his own beguiling marionettes, said, "People used to be ashamed to like puppets but they don't apologize today."

In person, Bil looks like what he is—a native of Grand Island, Nebraska. But, he's a pixie beneath his rugged exterior and his puppets are as unusual as the spelling of his name and as varied as his witty imagination. Bil started his training with Tony Sarg. Then he had his own show at the Chicago World's Fair and went on with it in vaudeville, nightclubs, Broadway theaters and films. He was ready for television before it was even invented.

Cora and Bil Baird were married in '37. She was a young actress but she soon added puppet strings to her bow and became a talented partner. The Bairds have always lived under the same roof as their workshop so their son and daughter had the most enviable playground in the whole wide world.

Regarding a Baird family line, Bil said:

"There is a maxim in the marionette business that if you put on a really good show, no one notices the strings . . . In our house, if anyone becomes pretentious or takes himself too seriously, we say: *'Your strings are showing!'* "

From Edgar Bergen

While he was growing up, Edgar Bergen expected to
become a doctor. Ventriloquism was just for fun until
high school days, when Edgar saved up $35 and bought

a wooden dummy that he named Charlie McCarthy. With Charlie draped on his knee, Edgar found that he could earn money entertaining at parties and by the time he started studying medicine at Northwestern University, wise-cracking Charlie was paying the tuition. From there, it was on stage for the two of them, in vaudeville and nightclubs.

In '36, Rudy Vallee convinced Edgar that radio listeners could enjoy his act even though they couldn't watch him. Rudy was right and the flip humor that Edgar wrote and delivered in Charlie's voice "mowwwed 'em down." He became the best known ventriloquist in the world and the only one to have a cover story by *Time Magazine*.

There were films, too, and when television came along, Edgar added to his range of writing and voice-throwing with the yokel, Mortimer Snerd, and the spinster, Effie Klinker. They all appeared on the Bergen TV quiz show *Do You Trust Your Wife?*

Mr. Bergen is married to the beautiful ex-Powers model, Frances Westerman, and they have a daughter, Candice. They also have a remark for anyone who takes himself too seriously. Here is how Edgar tells it.

"When Candice was about three years old, I would put her on one knee and Charlie on the other and they had many amusing conversations. She had such genuine acceptance of Charlie as a human being that I decided I was either a marvelous ventriloquist or she was a little stupid.

"I finally pressed my luck too far when I said, 'Isn't it wonderful how Charlie can talk?' She said, 'Yes it is, Daddy, *but you do move your lips!*'"

From Myra Waldo

Myra Waldo is quick-witted, bright and very pretty. She writes on travel and cooking—both of which she herself does in great style. Her cookbooks are best sellers and range from gourmet recipes to kitchenette quickies. Her Travel Guides, to Europe and to the Orient, tell all—how to go, where to stay, what to see, eat, buy. At the hairdresser's one day, a woman said, "Oh, Miss Waldo, we're going to the Orient. I haven't had a chance to get your book but would you tell me what to take along?" Miss Waldo smiled sweetly. "Money," she said.

Myra is married to an attorney, Robert Schwartz, who grins cheerfully when he is called Mr. Waldo. Myra and Bob have a comment they use about philandering husbands; Myra tells where it comes from.

"A man we know, who was in his late fifties, had a heart attack. This wasn't surprising because, even though he was married, he had never stopped leading the gay life of wine, song and lots of women.

"Bob went to visit him in the hospital and found him looking quite well and, as he put it, 'ready to have a little fun.' Bob said, 'You'd better take it easy.' 'Yes, I know,' the man answered, 'I've already had a long talk with my doctor. He told me that I must be careful not to over-exert myself and, above all, not to get overexcited. The doctor said I can resume—er—sex life, *but only with my wife!* "

Howard Whitman writes books on serious sociological subjects, among them, *Terror In The Streets, Terror In The Cities, Tell Your Child About Sex.* But after Mr. Whitman started appearing on television, it was easy to see that under his professorial exterior lies a budding actor.

This story bears out that theory. Mr. Whitman said, "When anyone in our family starts taking himself seriously, we have a little remark that lets out the hot air.

"We've been living in Westport, Connecticut, for some years but when we first left our New York apartment for the suburbs I felt like a country squire. I bought a couple of horses and our small daughter Connie often went riding with me across the fields and through the woods.

"Sometimes I let my imagination run wild and I would hold forth to Connie—and rather dramatically, I thought—on the Western plains, the mountain ranges and the arduous goals of the pioneers. Little Connie seemed to be a rapt listener.

"One crisp autumn day we were riding through a valley between two wooded knolls. There was a loneliness about the place that was exciting—just the trees in their solitude and the crackling and snapping of twigs beneath the horses' hoofs. I turned in the saddle and announced, 'Connie! We're up in the Canadian Wilds—we may not see a soul for days. We're lost—together—in the wilderness of the Great Northwest!'

"Connie gave me a quizzical look and explained, patiently, *'But, Daddy, this is Westport.'*"

From Mary Blunt

Did you ever find yourself in the hot seat of an embarrassing moment—tongue tied? Here is a line that came from Mary Blunt, Assistant Curator of the Buten Museum of Wedgwood, in Philadelphia, and she is undoubtedly the prettiest Fine Arts expert we've ever met.

Some time back, while Mary was in New York at an art show, she and an attractive man were introduced. The meeting was brief but there was immediate attraction and after Mary returned home, the New Yorker followed up with a charming letter. She answered. He sent flowers; then telephoned saying how anxious he was to see her again and suggested that he come to Philadelphia the next day to take her to lunch.

There was an electric excitement about the date when they met at Bookbinder's famous old restaurant. But when they were seated, there was an awkward pause. After all, they hardly knew each other. Mary nervously fumbled for a cigarette and her new beau whipped out his Zippo lighter. Forgetting that he had just filled it, he pressed hard and—whoosh—singed off her eyelashes. He looked at her tearing eyes; gulped miserably and croaked, *"How do you like me so far?"*

From Art Buchwald

Written humor has such a rare, precious quality that few authors can be consistently witty. Art Buchwald is one of the few. His columns are based on a wide variety of subjects—politics, people, news notes, small everyday happenings—yet they are unfailingly amusing. Very frequently they are so hilariously funny that they live for years. As an example, no one who ever read the Buchwald column on wine tasting has ever forgotten it!

For a number of years, Ann and Art Buchwald and their three children lived in France where Art's material was released through the Paris office of the *Herald Tribune*. Now they are living in Washington, D. C., which explains the title of one of his recent books *I Chose Capital Punishment.*

In families there are many times when a decision must be made but there are two different opinions on what is best to do. The Buchwalds have a way of ending such discussion. One of them just asks, *"Which St. Francis?"* Here is how Art explained the line. He said:

"It goes back to the story of the hard-luck guy who had nothing but trouble. Finally he jumped out of an airplane with two parachutes—neither one worked. As he fell through the air, he yelled 'St. Francis, St. Francis, help me!' and a hand reached out of the clouds; grabbed him by the collar and held him safe in midair.

"Then a deep voice from the sky spoke and asked, 'Were you calling St. Francis of Assissi or St. Francis of Xavier?' The man screamed: 'Xavier!' The voice said, 'Sorry' as the hand opened and let him drop."

You've probably heard the expression "A comedian's comedian." In show business, this is a tender accolade to an entertainer whose wit has gained the fond admiration of his fellow performers. George Burns is a comedians' comedian and one of his closest friends is Jack Benny. They swap stories, play highly competitive gin rummy, taunt each other's golf game and are frequent lunch companions.

If you have a family member or friend who always prefers what someone else has ordered in a restaurant, you'll enjoy this story, just exactly as George Burns told it:

"Jack Benny and I were eating in a restaurant and Jack is kind of peculiar—no matter what you order, he likes it. I said, 'I'll have some pot roast' and Jack said, 'I'll have some beef stew.'

"When the orders came, Jack looked at my pot roast and asked, 'Would you like some of my beef stew?' I said, 'No, because you'll want some of my pot roast.'

"The next day we ate together again. This time Jack ordered pot roast and I ordered beef stew. When we were served, he looked at my beef stew and asked, 'Would you like some of my post roast?' I said, 'No, because you'll want some of my beef stew.'

"The third day we both ordered beef stew and when it came Jack asked, 'Would you like some of my beef stew?' and I said: 'No, because you'll want some of my beef stew.' "

From Johnny Carson

You must see Johnny Carson to get the full tingle of
his mischievous wit. It takes the combination of his clean-
cut good looks, relaxed manner, innocent expression and

his humor. He may say, "We'll be back in a minute—turn your blanket on 'low' and put your husband on 'hold'." Maybe that isn't funny but when Johnny grins and says it, viewers whoop with delight.

Johnny was accused of too much "blue" innuendo and he said, "A smirk or a leer can make anything offensive. We're on late when you would assume that children are asleep. If you can't do something provocative now and then, the show would be pretty dull."

When Johnny came out of the Navy, he went to the University of Nebraska. Two years after graduation, he had a daily local T V show in Hollywood. Groucho, George Burns, Fred Allen and other big stars were his fans. They'd drop in and appear for free—even Jack Benny. His first network break came when Red Skelton was injured and Johnny substituted with only two hours' notice. Then he had his own national show, did guest appearances and was M.C. on *Who Do You Trust?* Four months after he succeeded Jack Paar on *The Tonight Show*, the old sky-high ratings rose by another half-million viewers!

The Carsons live in New York and Johnny tells this story about one of their favorite family comments.

"We have a standard answer when anyone, including my three boys, asks for a smaller portion than he has been served. It comes from Lindy's restaurant on Broadway where the waiters are famous for their answers.

"One night a guest ordered a demi-tasse and the waiter brought a large cup of coffee. The guest complained, 'But I ordered a demi-tasse! . . .' The waiter shrugged, '*So drink a little!*'"

From Norton Mockridge

The Norton Mockridge column has variety of flavor. Sometimes Mr. Mockridge writes about the city scene, sometimes he interviews celebrities—at times he just ruminates—but he is always amusing. His favorite subject, however, is the theater. To tell the truth, he is a thwarted thespian whose writing is better than his acting.

The Mockridges have two sons and a daughter and loads of family remarks. This one, Norton says, "Can stop the kind of argument that has degenerated into a see-saw of 'It is!' 'It isn't'! . . ." The line came from a conversation and this is the way he overheard it.

"A young man wearing a yellow raincoat and a green porkpie hat and a young lady wrapped in an imitation leopard coat were sitting next to me in a Lexington Avenue subway. The girl asked, 'You swear you'll tell me the truth?'

" 'I swear it, honey,' he answered, 'I swear it, I tell ya.'

" 'You really swear you'll tell me the truth?'

" 'Honest, I swear it, I tell ya—I swear it on the Bible—on my grandmother's grave! I SWEAR it!'

" 'Well,' said the girl, *'I won't believe you!' "*

There was sincere, deep mourning when Zachary Scott died in '65. He was so talented, so well liked, and, so young.

He and Ruth Ford were married in '52 and one of their many common bonds was admiration for William Faulkner's writings. In particular, Zachary Scott was determined to have the Faulkner play, *Requiem For A Nun* produced on Broadway. It had been expressly written for Ruth Ford, who came from Mr. Faulkner's home state of Mississippi. Ironically, the play had been acclaimed in England, France and ten other countries before Mr. Scott succeeded in having it open in New York. Ruth Ford said, "Zachary's been extraordinary in his dedication. All these years he's put this play first—before anything else. I doubt the money he's lost in other things—movies, television and the stage, too, could be calculated."

Just before Mr. Scott's illness, we met Ruth and her husband at an opening. We chatted and I happened to mention my brand new plan to collect family lines. Zachary said, "That's a good idea. Everyone has family remarks, I'll tell you one of ours.

"Ruth and I use an expression that means 'Never again! . . .' It comes from the time we were all having dinner with my grandmother. She was a Southern lady with a soft voice—but she could make sharp, barbed comments.

"I mentioned that a neighbor, newly separated from his shrewish wife, might be returning to her. . . Grandmother sniffed and disagreed. She said, *'One taste of a green gourd is enough!'* "

From Eddie Sherman

Eddie Sherman is the Walter Winchell of Honolulu but it took him a long time to get there.

Eddie was a young comedian working in Boston nightclubs when Pearl Harbor crashed into the news. He tried to enlist and when he was turned down because of an arm injury, he went to Honolulu and worked in a sheet metal defense plant for four years. He made a brief return to Boston but the Aloha lure was so strong that he came back to Hawaii. He was dead broke but ambitious. One idea kept recurring . . . there wasn't any "item" type of column in the daily paper and Eddie missed that kind of reading. So he took his idea to the editor of the *Honolulu Advertiser* who finally agreed to let him try— at five cents an inch. His first column netted him thirty-five cents.

A few years later, the column was beginning to mature and Eddie went to interview a visiting show business celebrity. Peggy Ryan was a dancer spending a vacation in Hawaii after finishing a movie. It was love at first sight and Eddie proposed a week later. As time went on, Peggy and Eddie adopted a little Korean orphan and Eddie's mother, Bessie, was so ecstatic at becoming a grandmother that she, too, came to Honolulu. Bessie speaks with a very strong Jewish accent but you can love a baby in any language and Bessie adored her little slant-eyed grandson, Shawn. It was from Bessie that Eddie acquired his favorite line of endearment for Peggy.

It seems that Bessie was wheeling Shawn in his carriage and a lady stopped to admire the cooing baby. Then she looked from the smiling little Korean face to Bessie's features and asked, "Are you the baby sitter?"

Bessie was indignant. "Baby sitter! I am the grandmother—this is my son's baby."

"Oh!" said the lady, "then your son married an Oriental?"

"Oriental? *Bad enough she's Irish!*"

From Jack Albertson

Jack Albertson, who won a Tony Award for his performance in *The Subject Was Roses* said, "There are always emergencies in the theater, especially before a show opens. If everything looks black and hopeless and anyone wails, 'What do you think we ought to do?' it reminds me of this incident.

"It happened back in the 40's when I was brand new in the theater and I became involved with a show called *Allah Be Praised*. The author was a Hollywood writer and, as soon as rehearsals started, it was easy to see that we were in trouble. But the writer wouldn't let anybody touch his precious script.

"Our producer was Alfred Bloomingdale, whose family owned the big Bloomingdale's department store. He finally convinced the playwright that unless we could hire a good play doctor, we'd have a dead turkey on our hands.

"Various writers were called in; each took one look at the show and gave up. Then Bloomingdale pleaded with Cy Howard to help us with rewrites. Howard came to watch a run-through and took a seat alone, toward the back of the theater.

"Just before the end of the play, Bloomingdale spotted Cy Howard sneaking out. He ran after him, grabbed him by the arm and said, 'But, Cy, you saw the show!'

"Cy Howard nodded. 'I did.'

"Bloomingdale asked, 'What do you think I ought to do?'

"Howard answered, *'Keep the store open nights.'* "

From Joan Crawford

Joan Crawford is far lovelier now than when she was a young starlet. Also, her recent performances were highly praised by critics. But she considers her acting career to be only a small part of her present life. As a Director of Pepsi-Cola and Frito-Lay, Joan has become their best goodwill ambassador. Her other interests are the National Association for Mental Health, the Heart Fund, the project HOPE and the USO, which she serves as a Vice-President.

Joan has twin daughters, Cynthia and Cathy. All three of them like pretty clothes and they have a favorite comment they make when they start discussing "what to wear." Joan tells the background of the remark.

"Our family fashion line comes from the story of the little girl who was always fussing with her clothes and wanting something new to wear.

"Her mother decided that such vanity had gone far enough and she sat down to have a heart-to-heart talk with the child. She explained that little girls have many responsibilities ahead and that they should not think so much of their clothes and appearance. She said, 'Imagine dear, some day you'll be grown-up and you'll get married and have children of your own!'

"Somehow this subject went further than the mother had planned and before she knew it, her little girl's questions had led the talk well into the facts of life.

"When the mother explained the 'planting of the seed,' the little girl's eyes grew big and round. She sat quietly for a moment—obviously she was thinking very seriously of what she had just heard. When she spoke, she asked, 'But, Mother, *what does a girl wear for a thing like that?*' "

From Dick Clark

When Dick Clark's show, *American Bandstand,* first hit America's television screens, it was an overnight sensation. Teen-agers all over the country tuned in and since they are the keepers of the home dials, Dick Clark became a household name and face. The show still has a fiercely devoted following—so does the daily Clark TV program called *Where The Action Is.*

Dick inherited his charm from his popular mother, Julie, and from his handsome father, Richard, Sr., who used to run a local radio station in upstate New York. Dick was boy-of-all-work around the station so he learned the broadcast side of show business young, and fast.

The Clarks have a special family way of saying "I don't know what you're talking about." They deliver their line in a nasal, squeaky twang. . . Here is Dick's story.

"Our remark comes from my great grandfather. The old gentleman was mighty hard of hearing and one day, seated at the family dinner table, my father said, 'Heard that Charlie is going to marry Jane Whitehouse.' Great Grandpa piped up, *'Who d'ja say is moving their out-house?'* "

From Eli Wallach

Eli Wallach doesn't like to be called a "method actor" because the term has become hackneyed. But that's what he is—for he lives, breathes and actually becomes every character he portrays. If you've seen him on Broadway or in films, for example, as the unforgettable opportunist in *Baby Doll*—you'll understand why he has been honored with both American and British Awards.

Eli is married to actress Anne Jackson, who has her own favorite family story in this book. They live in an old fashioned New York apartment where there is plenty of room for their three children and for Eli's irrepressible exuberance. They spend their brief holidays in a house near the ocean in East Hampton. The Wallachs have an unusually close family relationship and, as Eli's story points out, for an actor, this isn't easy. Here is how he tells it.

"During the past ten years I've wandered over most of the world on movie assignments . . . Hollywood, Mexico, Italy, England, France and even Cambodia and Japan. Though Anne is a dramatic star who understands an actor's career, separations are very difficult. But what really brings me home each time as fast as I can make it, is when Anne repeats a remark made by our youngest daughter, Katherine.

"Katherine asked, 'Mommy, when is Daddy coming home?'

"Anne's eyes filled to the brim. 'I don't know,' she answered, 'Daddy is far, far away, making a movie.'

"Katherine thought this over. Then she asked: *'Mommy, why don't we have two Daddies*—one to make movies and the other to stay home!' "

Anne Jackson is a superb actress and her most recent performance on Broadway as the leading lady of *Luv* brought glowing reviews from all drama critics. She is married to Eli Wallach and has taken three brief pauses in her acting career when she produced their children, Peter, Roberta and Katherine.

Anne's favorite line comes from a true happening and she quotes it whenever Eli turns thrifty. She said:

"I think that most people who are saving and economical were brought up that way. Thrift becomes a habit and even when there is no reason to skimp, it's hard to change.

"This took place when Eli had his first big break. He had just opened in a hit Broadway play and he had also signed a lusciously fat film contract for a new picture.

"Glowing with success, we sat in the kitchen and talked of the future. Eli made himself a cup of tea and asked, politely, 'Do you want some?' I shook my head and he dropped the used tea bag in the wastebasket.

"We continued our discussion about the film, the marvelous salary and Eli started to outline what it would mean to us. I gave a big, happy sigh and said, 'I've changed my mind. I'd like some tea.' Without pausing in his talk, Eli got up, took the tea bag from the wastebasket, put it in a cup and started to pour hot water over it.

"Aghast, I demanded, '*Now that we're rich, can't I have my own tea bag?*' "

From Robert L. Green

Robert L. Green is not the kind of man you call Bob. He's too dynamic for diminutives. Mr. Green is the fashion authority on *Playboy Magazine* and is the founder and director of the Caswell-Massey Awards that are coveted in the men's clothing industry. Though he doesn't like the term, he is known as the Voice of Fashion and his opinions have often determined red or black ink entries in a manufacturer's ledgers.

In person he is charming and witty, as you may know if you have heard him being interviewed on radio or television. At dinner parties he can swing his conversation from right to left in several languages, so he is a great catch as a guest. But he isn't caught very often as he likes to entertain and has a town house of his own, a farm in Bucks County and a villa at Cap D'Antibes. Also, he is a Cordon Bleu graduate and that causes a hostess to pause. With all these dazzling credits, it is pleasant to realize that Robert has no use for folderol or pretense. Here is one of his favorite stories.

"Snobbish little affectations can be irritating, or, you can laugh them off. This is a line that dismisses such nonsense.

"A young girl from the Middle West was presented to a pompous dowager from the Back Bay regions of Boston. The dowager asked, patronizingly, 'Where are you from?' and the girl answered in her Mid-Western twang, 'I'm from Iowa.'

"There was a moment of silence; then the great lady spoke: '*In Boston, we call it Ohio.*'"

From Monty Morgan

Monty Morgan has been producing *Girl Talk*, the TV show starring Virginia Graham, since it started in May '62. Monty says, "Count it up, five days a week, and it's a lot of talk!" It's a lot of "girls," too, and Monty has a talent for choosing combustible combinations of guests. Between Monty's choice and Virginia's skill, the shows bring out the beast as well as the best. TV viewers love the claw in back of the purr from such unions as Jolie Gabor with Margaret Truman; Betty Friedan (*Feminine Mystique*) with Hermione Gingold. They also write in, by the truckload, with discussions such as "Should parents walk nude in front of their children?", "Can a young woman really love an older man?"

Monty wanted to be an actor but before he had a chance to try, he was in the Army for five years. Then he did go to Hollywood briefly but impatiently turned to television and within a few years, was Associate Producer for Jack Paar, then producer for Merv Griffin, then— *Girl Talk*.

Recently, a writer, who was doing a magazine story on Monty, followed that one-man dynamo around on a typical working day. After it was over the writer said, "It's a good thing you don't own a restaurant or you'd be doing the dishes now!"

Monty has a favorite expression that he uses to end the endless arguments that come along when a television show is being put together. Here is how he explains it.

"In Romain Gary's autobiography, he told about the time he was an aviator and leaving for the war. His mother, a Jew, clung to him tearfully. Finally she clutched him in her arms once more and drew the Sign of the Cross with her finger on his forehead. . . He protested, 'But Mama, we're Jewish!' His mother shrugged and said, *'It can't hurt!'* "

Most of our great clowns started, as Bert Lahr did, in vaudeville and burlesque. It takes courage, talent and sweat of the brow to succeed in those tough fields of entertainment. Mr. Lahr has been a big time star ever since he appeared in the '28 Broadway musical show, *Hold Everything*. His exquisite sense of timing; his rubber-faced grimaces and his burbling cries are all well-known to theater, movie and TV audiences but his appeal is always fresh and engaging.

There is close kinship between comic and dramatic ability, well proven when Bert Lahr appeared in Beckett's *Waiting for Godot*. Yet the success that Mr. Lahr especially treasures is that he was able to wring laughs from his hard-boiled mates of World War I, when he was a Seaman 2nd Class in Uncle Sam's Navy.

Mr. and Mrs. Lahr live in the same comfortable apartment on upper Fifth Avenue that they have had since their children were youngsters. Mrs. Lahr is a beautiful woman who directs her energies to her home and to voluntary social service work.

The Lahrs have a favorite line that they quote whenever there is a disappointing postponement of plans. Bert Lahr tells the story.

"An actor, returning from his wife's funeral, went to his usual hang-out—the Lambs' Club. A friend tried to console him; patted him on the shoulder and said, 'Buck up, old man, I know it's tough. Give it a little time. Time heals all. . . .' The bereaved one brushed away a tear and sighed, *'But what'll I do for tonight?'* "

From Mimi Benzell

Mimi Benzell once wanted to be a doctor but no one encouraged her ambition—she was seven years old at the time. Instead, she studied piano until a severe case of pneumonia interfered. Mimi said, "I was too weak to resume piano lessons but my teacher didn't want to lose a pupil and she urged me to try voice. I didn't study seriously until I was eighteen. Two years later, I was singing at the Met."

Mimi's full, rich voice and her beguiling face and figure made her a joy to hear and see. But, during the five years of her important operatic career, she always had a hankering for popular music and finally began swinging the classics in smart supper clubs. She also was a frequent TV guest, starred in a Broadway show and by '66, was starting her third year in radio as hostess of *Luncheon With Mimi.*

Miss Benzell is married to Walter Gould, they have a son and daughter and a house in Long Island. Though her childhood fancy for becoming a doctor is long past, Mimi reads all medical news with avid interest and when an ailment shows up in the family, she earnestly suggests remedies. Her bent for "practicing without a license" amuses her husband. Mimi says:

"If Walter isn't feeling well and I suggest something for him to take, he's apt to answer, '*Shall I take it before or after?*'

"That comes from the story of a young woman who went to the doctor and said she'd like to know how she could be absolutely sure of not becoming pregnant. The doctor leaned back in his chair, smiled gently and said, 'It's very simple—just drink a half glass of orange juice.'

"She answered, 'Why, doctor, that's wonderful!' Then she thought for a moment and asked, 'Shall I take it before or after?' He said, 'Instead!' "

From Goodman Ace

Goodman Ace started as a serious drama critic in
Kansas City when he was still a teen-ager. But, he
changed to humor soon after and started writing *Easy*

Aces, a radio series that he and his wife Jane broadcasted for thirteen years. Jane played a lovable character whose lines, written by Mr. Ace, were marvels of confusion . . . "The way he treats her is abdominal . . ." "You could have knocked me down with a fender . . ." "In the ghetto where they have those old testament houses."

Later, Goody Ace became a top TV comedy writer with the best of the Berle, Caesar and Como shows to his credit. Readers know him for his sharp, witty columns in the *Saturday Review* and for his books. The newest, *The Fine Art of Hypochondria* is scheduled for the fall of '66.

Because Mr. Ace is well-known, he is often greeted by strangers and he always gives a cordial hello so their feelings won't be hurt. But Jane can tell when Goody is faking and she murmurs, *"Hello there, Kansas City."* Mr. Ace tells the origin of that family remark.

"Jane and I had been away from Kansas City about a year, having come to New York to do *Easy Aces*. A man hailed me in the lobby of a hotel, 'Hello there, Kansas City. . . .' I didn't recognize him but I said, 'Hello. Glad to see you again.'

" 'Remember me?' he asked. . . . 'Sure,' I lied. . . . 'Who am I?' he demanded.

"I told him I didn't remember his name but his face was familiar, which it wasn't. He laughed. 'I thought you didn't know me.' Then he told me his name. I still didn't know him but he kept me there, chatting about the old home town.

"Finally he said, 'You know who else is here in New York from Kansas City? He used to work on the paper back home and he's here doing a radio show—Goodman Ace.' "

From Florida's Gold Coast

Arthur has a standard remark that he makes when he considers that I am overloaded with luggage on a trip. It comes from an experience we had in Palm Beach some years ago.

While there, we met a charming, middle-aged Frenchman. He owned a famous collection of paintings and could very well afford his expensive hobby. That evening he introduced us to his new bride—a young, curvaceous Southern girl and it was obvious that he doted on her.

Strolling on the beach the next day, we met his little Sugar Plum. She was wearing a teenty weenty bathing suit . . . plus a handsome aquamarine, ruby and diamond star hanging from a slender chain. The star rested just above the V of her low, low neckline and it was impossible to overlook it.

Arthur said to her, "That's a beautiful necklace." "Oh, the-uss," she drawled in her Southern accent, as she fingered the jeweled pendant, "when Ah travel, *Ah just take a few l'il things to wear to the beach.*"

From Jean Carroll

Jean Carroll has been headlined repeatedly on every major T.V. variety show. She has been Ed Sullivan's guest comedienne sixty times! Her humor—always fresh and timely—is delivered rapid fire, in what sounds like a Brooklyn accent. Where was she born? . . . Paris, France.

Recently, a reporter who was interviewing her about various nightclub appearances asked, "Which spots shall I mention?" Miss Carroll told him, "You could mention two spots—black beauty marks on my left leg and thigh."

Jean said that in her family, anyone who imagines he has done a great job can be brought back to reality with three words *"You should live."* Here is the story.

"My mother had never seen me on a stage and I per-suaded her to come to the old Loew's Commodore on 14th Street in New York, where I was singing, dancing and doing impressions with a band act. I really wanted to impress her and I tried so hard that I almost knocked myself out. But I felt I had never been better so when she came backstage to my dressing room, I was bubbling. 'Well, Mom, how did you like it?'

" 'The movie was very good—very nice.'

" 'Mom, I'm not asking about the movie. . . .'

" 'The seats were very comfortable.'

" 'Mom, for once in your life, give me a direct answer. How did you like *me*?'

"She looked at me as though she'd never seen me be-fore . . . 'You? *You should live* to get the applause that singer in the second act got!' "

From Peter Lind Hayes

Peter Lind Hayes joined his mother, Grace, in her vaudeville act when he was nine years old. He never left show business except for World War II when he enlisted in the Army Air Force.

Peter met his beautiful blonde wife, Mary Healy, in Hollywood. Mary was in films, fresh after winning a "Miss New Orleans" contest. Since then, they have played together in theaters, nightclubs, on radio and TV. They cruise together, too, in their thirty-five-foot Queen Mary III, along with their children, Peter and Cathy.

Big Peter is a nut on gadgets. He has rigged an intercom between the house and the boat, between the house and the golf course—where he shoots in the low 70's—has installed amplifiers so he can talk on the phone from anywhere in the room and has placed secret touch-spots so that lamps turn on mysteriously. Mary doesn't have inventive quirks but, as Peter says, "She is funniest when she doesn't mean to be. Our whole family likes to remind her of this one . . .

"An old Air Force buddy showed up at our house one evening and our reminiscing dragged on and on. About midnight, Mary got to yawning openly. Around two o'clock she started tapping her foot and at three, she suggested that my old buddy either stay for the night or pack up his memories and slip away.

"He took her unveiled hint and as he tipsily reached the front door, Mary pulled herself together, politely shook his hand and said, heartily, 'Good-night, *I'm nice to have met you!*' "

From Arthur Treacher

Captain Arthur Veary served in the British Army during all of World War I. By the time he was discharged, he had completely lost interest in returning to the study of law and decided to try the stage. He made his London debut in the chorus of a musical revue—as Arthur Treacher. He had graduated to more important roles when the Shuberts saw him and offered him a Broadway contract. After appearing in a number of plays, he went to the Hollywood Playhouse and was soon spotted by film scouts.

"Type casting" is a Hollywood habit and after Mr. Treacher had appeared as a butler in several consecutive films, the director said, "You look bored." "I am," he answered, and the director suggested that he try playing the part that way. That started his popular characterization of the haughty major domo who served with such distinctive disdain. Mr. Treacher, however, is a versatile dramatic actor and has been well cast in Shaw plays, mysteries and comedies. TV viewers are currently enjoying him as co-host for Merv Griffin. He told us this story backstage.

"Now, I've never thought of myself as a tightwad. I'm just—let us say—rather careful. But I wish I had never told this incident to my family and friends because I've been bombarded with the line ever since.

"It happened on a very wet day when I was standing at 44th Street and 6th Avenue in New York waiting for a bus. . . . The bus pulled up, the driver opened the door and as I was about to climb in, he took one look at me and banged the door in my face as he yelled, '*You know you can afford a taxi, Arthur!*' "

Cardinal Samuel A. Stritch of Chicago had a little cousin named Elaine and he advised her parents to send her to the Sacre Coeur Convent for her schooling. They did and so she grew up to be an actress.

Elaine Stritch is a comedienne-singer who stopped the show with hot song numbers in *Angel In The Wings*, in *Pal Joey* and in *On Your Toes*. She is also a dramatic actress and gave terrific performances in *Bus Stop*, *Goldilocks* and other Broadway plays. She is seen, at frequent intervals, on television.

Offstage, Elaine is a good-looking, slender, well-dressed blonde with a breezy sense of humor. Here is one of her favorite family stories.

"When friends in show business are performing, they take it for granted that you'll be complimenting them. Sometimes I surprise them with a remark that once startled me.

"I was appearing in a television special that had been taped and I thought it would be fun to look at the show with my four-year-old niece. I was curious to see how she would react as she watched me on the screen, while I was sitting right next to her. And, to be honest, I also expected some wonderment and admiration.

"She was quiet as a mouse all during the show, right to the very end. Then I snapped off the set, turned on the lights and asked, 'Well, how did you like me in the show? . . .'

"She looked at me dolefully and complained: '*You never mentioned my name!*'"

From Dorothy Stickney

Dorothy Stickney's life story has more heart throb than any dramatic role she has ever played. She was born in Dickinson, North Dakota, which she says was "a small town with five saloons and a post office." When she was only three, she was almost blinded by corneal ulcers. Repeated operations brought only minor results. Later, a miracle seemed to come by itself when her eyesight returned.

But her handicap gave her a career. Because her dimmed vision kept her from preparing for college, Dorothy studied elocution and dancing. When she regained her sight, she tried out for the stage, landing dance jobs in vaudeville. She also played a Folies Bergere girl, with padded tights to camouflage her five-foot-two, thin as a whistle figure.

She met her future husband, Howard Lindsay, in summer stock. He was the director and Dorothy says, "Before Howard came along, I played by instinct." She then made her Broadway debut in '26 and married her coach the following year.

Dorothy and Howard had separate careers until '39, when they played the leads in the Lindsay-Crouse show *Life With Father*. That play grossed its first million in less than a year and turned out to be one of the greatest financial bonanzas that the theater has ever known.

The Lindsays have ease of communication. But—like other couples—they, too, have favorite family lines. Here is one they use when either of them regrets becoming involved in something.

"A comic named Harry Kelly, billed as 'The Deacon,' used to appear in a Prince Albert, a shabby top hat—and, he wore a solemn, sorrowful expression.

"In one restaurant scene, a waiter approached his table and asked, 'How is the soup? . . .' Kelly was silent for a moment; then turned his sad eyes to the waiter and answered, *'I'm sorry I stirred it.'* "

From Judith Crist

Judith Crist is the nationally syndicated motion picture critic whose sharp wit is the delight of her readers and whose influence is the fright of the movie industry. Since she is also an Associate Drama Critic, she is well qualified as film and drama commentator on the TV *Today* shows.

Judith and her husband, William, who is the New York representative for a number of liberal arts colleges, live in Manhattan with their son Steven. This family saying started soon after Steven was born. Here is the story—from Mrs. Crist.

"Whenever anyone makes a banal observation on something that is all too obvious, we quote a remark made by Miss Clare, the nurse who took care of our son when he was a baby.

"Miss Clare was a stickler for attire and she had starched chic when she aired little Steven in Washington Square. He was a golden-haired infant and, ensconced in his Rolls-Royce pram, aglow in baby blues and yellows, the two made a royal appearance.

"During the day, however, displaced Bowery bums also came to the Square and, try as she could, Miss Clare could not avoid them. One day, a whiskered, filth-encrusted, alcohol-sodden derelict draped himself on the bench next to her and proceeded to blow saloon fumes at her and Steven. Too terrified to move, Miss Clare smiled politely though apprehensively and his attention then moved to Steven.

"After a considered study of the baby, he turned back to Miss Clare and said, in tones of wonder, 'My God he's clean!' 'Well,' said Miss Clare as she rose to flee with the carriage, *'we wash him a lot!'* "

From William Davenport

William Davenport writes travel books of rare delight. They have a Mark Twain flavor and, here and there, Bill slips in a sly Rabelaisian touch.

Bill and his artist wife, Roselle, and their two children live in France. But one of their family lines started back in Hawaii when Bill was a professor of journalism at the University. Here is how he tells about it.

"In our house no one ever says Bon Voyage to me. When I leave on a trip, they all repeat what our son Tony said at the age of three, when we were still living in Aloha land.

"Back in Honolulu Roselle always paid all bills by check and she never seemed to remember to keep any petty cash around the house. So when the Good Humor man stopped by, the children came to papa.

"One morning at breakfast, I was called to come to the neighboring island of Maui to work with a movie company on location there. As I started to pack, little Tony burst into tears.

"Naturally I was deeply touched and quite flattered by such filial devotion and I tried to comfort him. 'Why, Tony, you mustn't cry.'

" 'But you're going away,' he wailed.

" 'I'll be back soon—so why are you crying?'

" 'Because,' he sobbed.

" 'Because WHY?'

" '*Who's gonna pay for the ice cream!*' "

From Frank Fontaine

Crazy Guggenham is crazy like a fox. The character named "Guggenham," seen for the past few years on the *Jackie Gleason Show*, was invented by a capable, hardworking performer, Frank Fontaine.

Mr. Fontaine has been in show business for over twenty-five years—he started in his parents' vaudeville act. At seventeen, when he married a young acrobatic dancer, he was on his own. He had a good baritone voice but it was a struggle to make a living with small nightclub bookings in and around Boston. He sang, told stories and did impersonations.

After three years of military service in World War II, Mr. Fontaine went to Hollywood and his rubber-face was seen in films starring Bing Crosby, Jane Wyman, Ann Sheridan and others. He had radio jobs, too, and on television, guest shots with Ed Sullivan and Jack Benny. Then came his lengthy association with Jackie Gleason.

Since the Fontaines have nine sons and two daughters, it is nice to realize that he has parlayed his efforts into a real pay-off.

Vic McLeod, well-known comedy writer, heard this one in the Frank Fontaine household. It is their automatic answer when any member of the family expresses a dislike for a food that is being served. It comes from the time that one cannibal said to another, "I don't like my mother-in-law." His friend answered, "*So just eat the noodles.*"

From Earl Wilson

Earl Wilson comes from Rockford, Ohio, and looks as guileless as a cherub. But, his syndicated column of humor and show business gossip has been running since '42 and he knows everybody's way around!

Earl's wit is seldom sharp but it's frequently salty. He had quips on the a, b, c of a maiden's form long before topless bathing suits busted into the news. Earl's Pearls, his Remembered Quotes and his deft paragraphs have a devoted following.

In the Wilson family—which means his B. W., Rosemary, and their son—anyone who shows off is called Mr. Le Bourget. Earl said:

"That comes from the time Rosemary and I made our first trip to Europe. We arrived at Le Bourget on a hot sticky day and found that the Hotel George V had sent a chauffered limousine with an assistant manager to greet us. I was perspiring, confused, worrying about the right tips for porters and though I was self-conscious about my Berlitz French, I was anxious to use it.

"Rosemary, dazzled with anticipation and the impressive welcome, caroled blissfully, 'Darling, just think— *this* is Le Bourget! . . .' I grabbed the manager's hand, pumped it up and down and stuttered, 'Je suis—je suis— oh nuts, *I'm terribly glad to meet you, Mr. Le Bourget.*'"

Ann Landers is the pen name of a five-foot-two, bantam weight champion who lands kayo punches with words. Her viewpoint, explained in her Sioux City drawl, is: "When you sit down and cry with people, you don't help them. Some people have to be shook—and Ah shakes them."

Married in '39 to Jules Lederer, she was a housewife for sixteen years and an active participant in community affairs. Then, with no previous newspaper or magazine writing experience, she turned out her first column for a twenty-six newspaper line-up. In less than a year she tripled that list and now her syndicated coverage is enormous. "I was lucky," she claims, "I was in the right place at the right time." She should add, "With the right talent."

Here is a line from Miss Landers that a husband can use when his wife appears in a frowsy get-up, such as curlers and shrunken slacks. It comes from this incident.

"A housewife found a badly leaking overhead pipe in the basement and rushed to phone a plumber. He said he couldn't get there until later but advised her to make a temporary patch and told her just how to do it.

"Down she went to the cellar with rags and tape and, not wanting to get her clothes soaked, undressed to the skin. She saw her son's football helmet on a shelf and clapped that on her head to keep her hair dry.

"Concentrating on the job, she didn't hear the gas man arrive to read the meter. But she heard him gasp and she wheeled around as he gulped and said, '*I hope your team wins, lady!*'"

Helen Hayes once said, "It's because I was pigeon-toed that I am an actress at all!" When she was only five, her mother sent her to a dancing school in Washington, D. C. to learn to walk gracefully. The Broadway producer, Lew Fields, stopped in to watch a recital; spotted Helen and said, "If that little girl ever wants to go on the stage, tell her to see me." When Helen was nine, her mother did take her to Mr. Fields' office and she was launched in his shows.

Later, she returned to Washington; graduated with honors from the Sacred Heart Academy and thereafter, her career was steadily glorified by one dramatic success after another. Her personal life was exciting, too. Witty as well as pretty, she became the darling of producers, writers and critics—including playwright Charles MacArthur whom she married in '28.

Miss Hayes' roles, Awards, and honorary degrees are an impressive history. She also made legal history when she became pregnant and won the right to leave the Jed Harris play, *Coquette* through the Act of God clause in her contract.

Helen Hayes has deep religious beliefs, as you can read in her book *A Gift of Joy*. She also has a salty sense of humor—as you can tell from her family line. The line is used when anyone talks of personal triumphs of long ago. Here is how Miss Hayes tells it.

"The story is about an old lady who went to confession. She quavered in her cracked, aged voice, 'Father, I have committed adultery.' The priest was shocked: 'What! I can hardly believe it—when did this happen?' The dear old lady answered, 'It was sixty years ago— *but I still like to talk about it.*'"

From Merv Griffin

When Merv Griffin filled in on *The Tonight Show* for the newly departed Paar, the M.C.'s host chair was known as the hot seat. Many a star expired in it. Merv, however, was hailed as an overnight success. He said ruefully, "Some overnight! I've been singing and performing for seventeen years. The only difference is that this is the first time I ever sat down during a show."

It's nice to see the *Merv Griffin Show* high in the top ratings because, besides being talented, he is such a charming, gracious person. He is married to a former comedienne; they have a small son, an old farm and this true story that took place on the homestead—just as Merv tells it.

"My wife's maiden name was Julann Wright but she has a knack for doing things wrong. Whenever Julann runs true to form, I like to remind her of the news headline she once made.

"Robert J. Williams of the *Philadelphia Bulletin* is a highly respected TV columnist and I was very pleased when he asked to do a Sunday feature about our farm.

"He arrived on a very misty day but said he wanted to look around and choose the spots to be photographed. After tramping through the wet fields, we were soaked and went back to the house where Julann hospitably offered to dry Mr. Williams' shoes.

"A short while later, I went to the kitchen for ice, smelled something burning and opened the oven door. There were Mr. Williams' shoes—black, charred and warped completely out of shape.

"The following Sunday the feature article appeared with the headline: '*NEVER, NO, NEVER GIVE MRS. MERV GRIFFIN YOUR SHOES!*' "

From The White House

The more important the man, the more he is subjected to caricature and lampoons. President Lyndon Baines Johnson has had a heavy share. His colorful speech, dramatic sense of political timing, his Texan background —even his initials—have made him an easy target and he has had to wince through a raft of parodies, some of doubtful taste. Most pungent may be this one . . .

"L. B. J. and Lady Bird were walking along the river bank and he asked her, 'Do you see anybody anywhere around?' She scanned the surroundings and said, 'No, I don't see anyone.' He asked, 'Are you sure there aren't any Secret Service men following us?' She looked again, even more carefully, and answered, 'No, I don't see a soul.' 'Well then,' he said, 'I'm going to try walking on that water just once more.' "

At home, however, no member of the Johnson family gets away with exaggerated conceit. At the first sign of swell-headedness, the magic antidote is the remark from this true happening. It is told by Lynda Bird.

"One day when Mother was shopping in a department store in Austin, she saw a lady who had worked very hard for years on my father's campaigns—she was a real party worker.

"Mother was in a great hurry and kept arguing with herself—should she take the time to go over and speak or should she just pretend she didn't see her. Of course, she finally went over and gave the lady a big hello. Well, the lady looked straight at Mother for a minute and then asked, 'Do I know you, dearie?' "

From Mike Wallace

Back in '56, Mike Wallace was the bogeyman of a TV show called *Night Beat*. A guest was placed in a hot, white spotlight and as Mike shot questions, viewers could see every pore and bead of sweat on the victim's face. But guests weren't paid to appear nor did anyone force them. So Mike must have had more fascination than a cobra. He also had enormous energy and did detailed research before facing a guest in the "hot seat."

Those days are over and Mike is back to his chief interest—the news. But many people still remember the night when gangster Mickey Cohen, pressed by Mike about his past, said, "I have killed no man that in the first place didn't deserve killing!"

On the lighter side, here is a Wallace family line explained by Mike.

"When I use salty language and my wife wants me to tone down, she repeats a remark once made by Mrs. Harry Truman.

"It came from the time that Mrs. Truman went to a Grange meeting in Independence, attended by farmers from nearby localities. She went with a friend of hers whose husband was the chief speaker that day.

"The topic was 'Conservation of the Soil' and the man was a forthright speaker with a clear, forceful voice. He ended by summarizing his points and then he pounded the stand in front of him as he said, 'Just remember—what you need is manure, manure—and more manure!'

"His wife was embarrassed and whispered to Bess Truman, 'Oh dear, I've been trying to get him to say fertilizer! . . .' Mrs. Truman whispered back, *'I've been trying to get Harry to say manure!'* "

The name Rod Serling has been evoked in many an argument on the value of television. To the statement: "Television is for morons!", the clinching answer can be: "What about Rod Serling's shows?"

When *Patterns* was shown in January '55, the playwright, Rod Serling, became an overnight success. He has maintained his high level with provocative, exciting TV plays and it's been far from easy. Writing is a tough craft but it's even tougher to get realism presented in a medium well guarded to protect a sponsor's sales in every region of the country. Rod, however, is a hard fighter!

In person, Rod is an engaging conversationalist, charming and witty. Here is a Serling family remark that Rod tells.

"When anyone in our household tells a long drawn-out tale, someone is sure to stop him with the line from this story.

"A well-known comedian, scheduled to entertain at a benefit dinner, was seated at the table of honor on the dais. Drinks were poured freely. After dinner, the toastmaster first called on the president of the organization to 'say a few words.' He turned out to be a dull speaker and he droned on and on. From the dais, the toastmaster watched the bored audience and suddenly noticed a few of the guests grinning and nudging each other. He looked around, saw that the comedian had gone soundly to sleep so he reached out surreptitiously with his gavel and tapped him to wake him up.

"The comedian stirred, then yelled, '*Hit me again—I can still hear him!*'"